KT-452-415

TWO THOUSAND YEARS

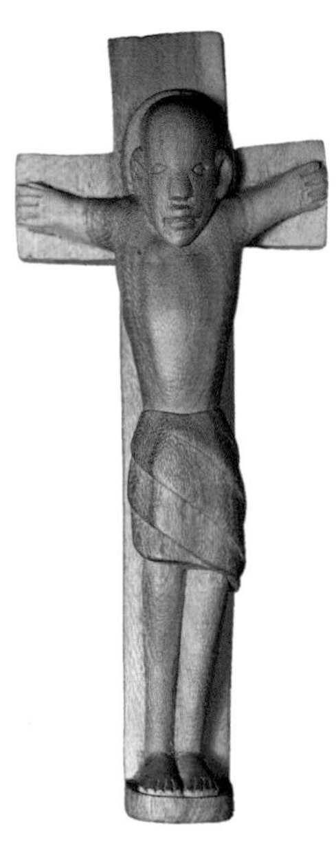

To Joyce, who made it possible

Two Thousand Years

The Second Millennium:
From Medieval Christendom to Global Christianity

Peter Partner

With a foreword by Melvyn Bragg

GRANADA
MEDIA

With thanks to Richard Thomson and Simon Cherry

First published in Great Britain in 1999
By Granada Media, an imprint of André Deutsch Limited,
in association with Granada Media Group.
76 Dean Street
London
W1V 5HA
www.vci.co.uk

A catalogue record for this book is available from the British Library.

ISBN 0 233 99666 4
Editorial Cover(to)Cover a.t.e.
Picture research by Sophie Seebohm
Book design © Design/Section
2000 Years titles logo © Hobbins Sides
Front cover images 3,4,7, 11, 14,15,16 & 17 © 1998 PhotoDisc, Inc

Printed in the UK by Butler & Tanner, London, and Frome, Somerset

1 3 5 7 9 10 8 6 4 2

Contents

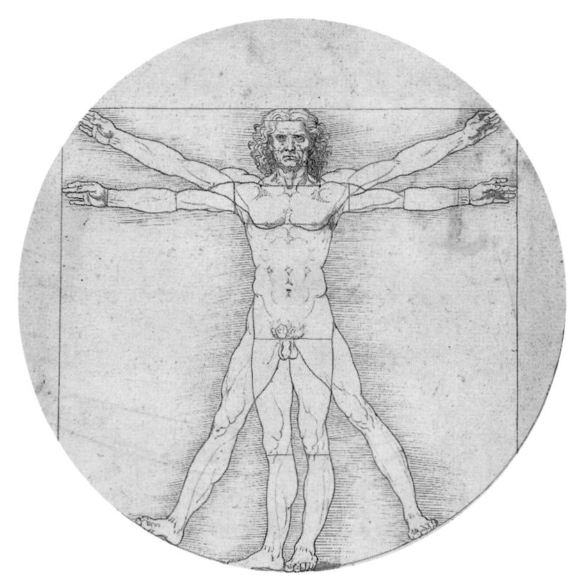

FOREWORD

It would not be difficult to present the second millennium of Christianity in terms just as melodramatic, bombastic and astonishing as the first.

This after all was the millennium that was soon riding into battle with one of its oldest enemies, Judaism, which itself was the ally of the biggest new threat to Christianity – Islam. Tension between these religions was matched by the tension between Rome and Constantinople within Christianity itself, their virulent feuds expressed in terms of theology which now seem bled of all passion (what was the status of the Holy Ghost?) but at that time carried the power of the sword. The Christian city of Constantinople (Byzantium), which had feared destruction from the armies of Islam, was ransacked by fellow Christians who had been launched on the Fourth Crusade from Venice.

And being the great sponge which has been one of its characteristics (just as being the great stone, impervious, has been another) Christianity absorbed learning – mathematics, medicine and many of the arts – from the Muslims, learning which was to transform the Western societies in which Christianity was now an integral and most essential part.

The massive divergent uses to which Christianity was put and the circumstances it inspired, continued on their spectacular way. In the thirteenth century for instance, wealthy, even opulent cathedral-building on a dazzling scale began to sweep through Christian countries resulting in works in stone and glass which still today have a grandeur scarcely matched since. Yet in the same century, the Cathars in southern France were preaching a stern unworldliness and found many converts, as did the wandering friars who continued in unbroken line from the apostles to preach 'leave all that thou hath and follow me'.

Below: Danse Macabre

The Crusades, like many other wars, were wars more often inspired and blessed by Christianity than averted or condemned. State Christianity had begun because Constantine gained victory in battle, a result he attributed to a visionary dream, and the association with battle continues up to the present century. In the fifteenth century the Western Church was divided against itself with two rival Popes – one in Rome and one in Avignon – and as the sailor warriors of the Western seaboard took the faith to new continents, the cross gave its blessing to guns and swords and conquests time and again. Christianity was a reinforcer of military power. Although, as always, many fine souls did good when most around them were evil, the alliance between the Church militant positioned to save souls at whatever cost, and the advanced European countries on the rampage for land, gold, loot of all kinds, yoked together a faith and colonialism that many thought more a pact made by Satan than any Jesus of Nazareth.

Intolerance was another unmistakable feature of this empire-serving, empire-building religion. Whether it was Luther's intolerance of the Jews and the Roman Catholics, or the Church's intolerance for science, or Christian rejection of the Enlightenment, Christianity fed the very worst in opposing the intellectual development of humankind. It commanded zealously in the name of the All-Powerful, All-Demanding, All-Knowing Invisible God to whom nothing was hidden. The only key was the life and teachings and texts that Christians alone held and believed should be held by everyone else.

Yet if nothing was too bad to do in the name of the Christian Father, the Son and the Holy Ghost, nothing was too good either. Christianity did indeed kow-tow to the European slavers who worked with the African slavers to provide the cheap labour for the New World. But Christianity was also the moral force that brought it to an end. Wilberforce and his friends have a place in history obscured by current understandable bruises and furies over slavery and ransom, but the fact that slavery was ended was due to the power of those carrying out the teachings of Christ.

Nor is it permissible to talk of Christianity without mention of a sect such as the Quakers, whose pacification and tolerance were a beacon difficult to see lit unless fuelled by the ethical commands of Christ. And individual lives, by the million, small unnoticed lives of kindness and goodness as well as ambitious philanthropic gestures, were again and again inspired by the wish to live up to the expectations set by the Christ of the Gospels and the Acts of the Apostles.

The works of art which owed Christianity everything from their existence and their execution to their force and persistence in the culture are literally countless. The cathedrals themselves, the stained glass of Chartres, the awesome simplicity of Durham Cathedral, the waves of stone from Notre Dame to the Sagrada Familia, these alone for some would vindicate the faith. But of course they are not alone; there are also the Passions and the Masses composed by musicians of genius, the story of Christ painted so often and so majestically. It is unnecessary to make a list. For 2,000 years, much of what has been, and remains, culture in various Western countries and civilizations and in the global Diaspora of the West can be related to the teachings and credo, the visible and invisible dynamism developed in bewildering variety from that one root planted by the Sea of Galilee.

It has had its opponents. Not only in Roman classical times and in the eighteenth-century Enlightenment, not only from Judaism and Islam and all the many faces of fanatical non-religious and pacific aetheistical positions, but also, again and again, from individuals who have dispersed and railed against its messages and its impact. Friedrick Nietzche for instance, famously announced that 'God is dead'. He detested its other-worldliness and found resentment at the heart of the religion: resentment of the world, of the body, of sex, of the vital intelligence, of everything strong and

Above: Quarrelling Cardinals

healthy. Even the Christians' love for their enemies, according to Nietzche, was only a tactic to ensure a quicker passage to eternal life.

But despite Voltaire, Nietzche, Darwin, Marx, Freud and thousands of dissenting voices gathering volume and power over the last 200 years in particular, Christianity still flourishes, though not in some of the countries it once did. But it is still a palpable force not least in the one remaining world empire – an empire as powerful as Constantine's Rome in the fourth century – in the United States of America. There the God of the New Testament and the God of Abraham still lives and the great Satan was seen until recently in Communism, itself inspired by another Jew, another rabbinical figure.

Nor is Christianity, even today when doubt is to be the new faith, bereft of intellectual defenders. An Oxford professor of philosophy, Lesjek Kolakowski, for instance, was recently described as one who 'belongs to the peaceful tradition of Christian thinkers who find in Christianity not a political or social programme or system of government but a way of life springing from two beliefs . . . the belief that Jesus the Redeemer appeared on earth in historic times in order to free us from evil from which we could not free ourselves, and the ability to remove hatred which follows from this belief'. Kolakowski himself has said, 'If God is dead, nothing remains but an indifferent void which engulfs and annihilates us'.

Above: The Sermon

At present Darwinians argue most persuasively against the Christian philosophers and teachers of the past and of the present, but the Christian agenda is still part of the lives we lead in this century. What part did Christianity play in the anti-Semitism that led to the Holocaust? Has Christianity helped to organize and enable the state, even the modern state, to become a machine for crushing individuals or has Christian faith fortified individuals against the juggernauts of state? Is wealth and its pursuit wholly inimical to a just society and where does the wealth of the Church fit in with the Sermon on the Mount? Will Darwin finally kill off the idea of the quest for a perfect society which we can see from Plato's *Republic* to Karl Marx's *Das Capital,* but most ferociously and relentlessly and often delightfully pursued in Christianity? And if science neither needs nor knows of a religious sense, where does the 'why' question, the spiritual need, the religious temperament, come from?

Christianity over this 2,000 years has magnetized history, thought and art; it has made coalitions out of contrary forces and yet bred and even cultivated centralism in itself. Its source and its power lie in resurrection even today. Witness the way it is absorbing the new discoveries of cosmology. It continues to strive to resurrect itself. It has never been afraid to preach and rely on the miraculous and its survival alone over 2,000 years must surely rank as some sort of miracle.

Melvyn Bragg, 1999

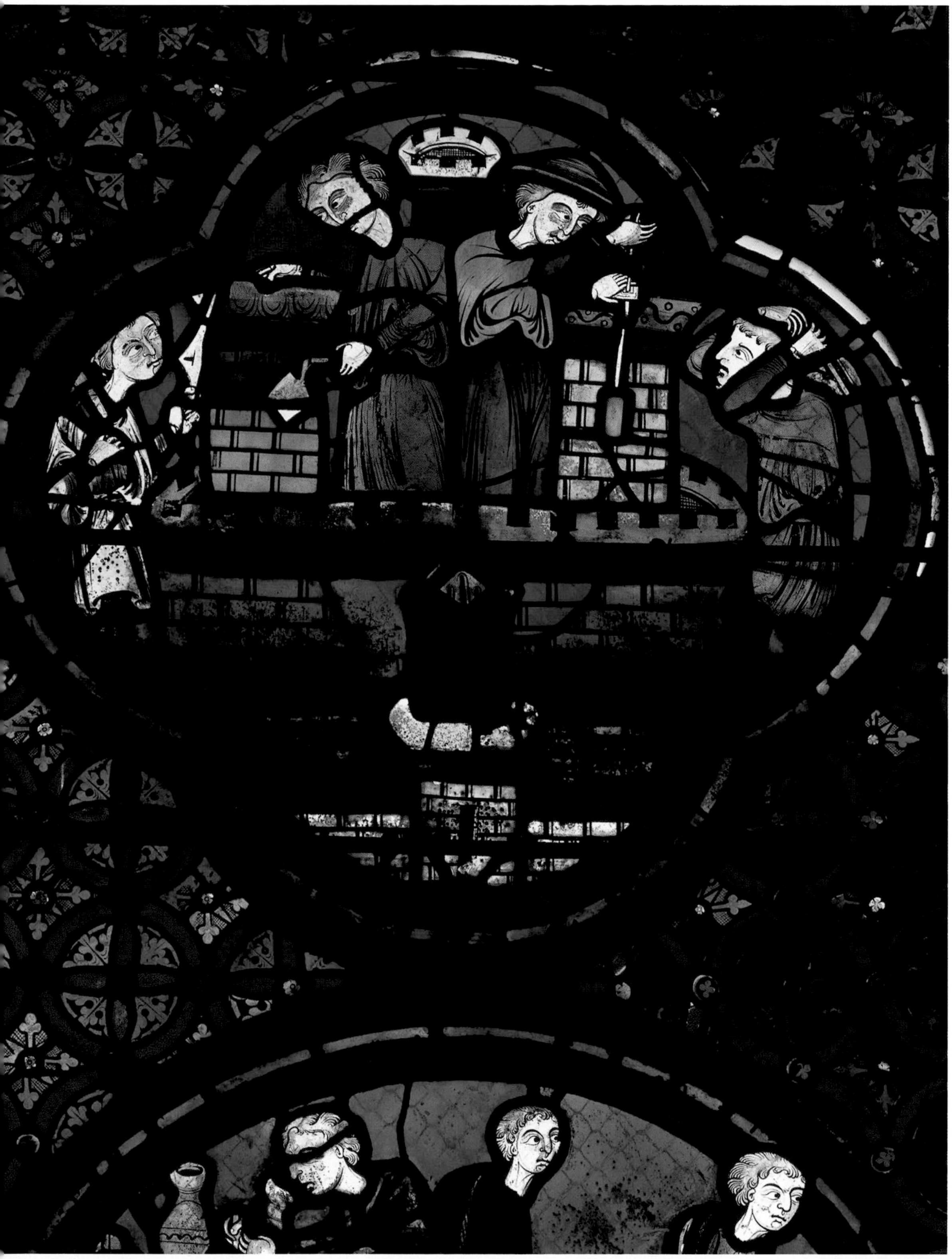

© Peter Willi, Cathedral of St Etienne, Bourges, France/Bridgeman Art Library

© British Library, London, UK/Bridgeman Art Library

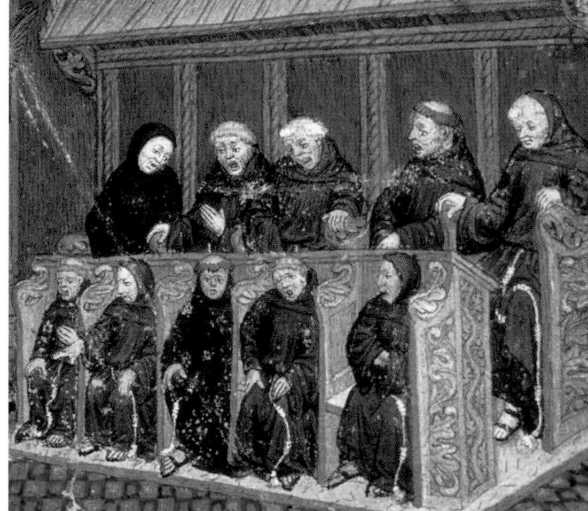

Above: Franciscan monks

Left: The masons of St Etienne, Bourges

to the legislators, and allowed by the popes only in the single instance of the Slav liturgy, probably translated by a Greek speaker from the Latin original used by Constantine and Methodios.

Conversions and Christendom

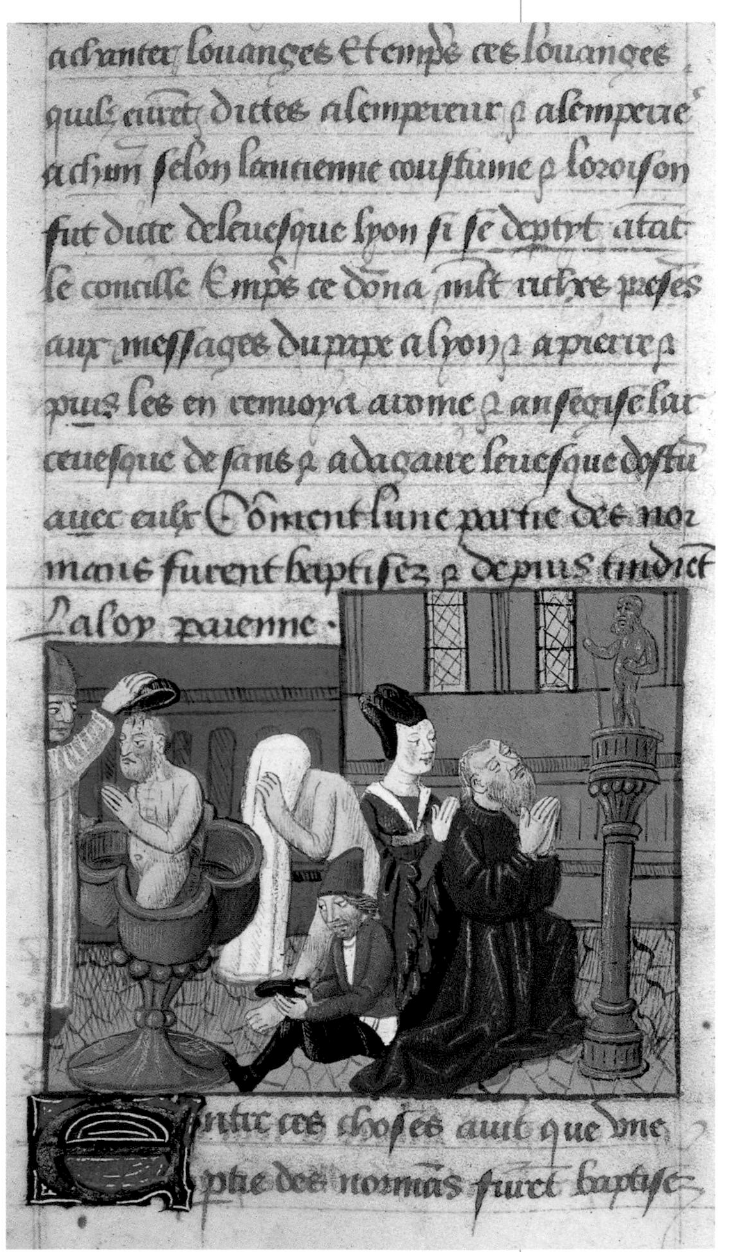

Above: The early fifteenth-century Chroniques des Bois *shows a Norman being baptized, apparently of his own free will. There was debate at the time about the advisability of baptism by force.*

The statements attributed to Jesus about preaching the news of salvation to all nations and making them his disciples (Matt. 28: 19; Mark. 16: 15) may seem unambiguous, even though the proclamation of the Gospel was also related to his second coming and to the end of the age (Matt. 24). Equally definite, or so it seemed to St Augustine of Hippo, was St Paul's rhetorical question to the Romans about the salvation of the Jews (Rom. 10: 14–15): how could they be saved without someone to spread the good news to them, who had been sent with that purpose? But, as has recently been emphasized,[1] the missionary impulse was not something built into Christianity that operated, as it were, automatically. By the early Middle Ages, Christianity was becoming a closed society. St Boniface's reluctance to launch the conversion of the Slavs from an east Frankish base was not an isolated phenomenon. It was axiomatic with the majority of learned Christians that Christ did not die for every man, but for the elect alone. It was not for many centuries, and after much hesitation, that mainstream Christianity emerged from that position.

Nor was there anything easily predictable about the manner of effecting the conversion, either as to its duration or as to its practical effect. In the long term, the converted peoples were to become part of a cultural entity that was by the eleventh century called Christendom, and which for clarity scholarship calls 'Latin' Christendom. The common liturgical language was not in every single case Latin, and religious changes in modern and relatively modern times have meant that 'Latin' refers to the historical origins of national churches, and not to the religious practice of today, which may be Catholic or Protestant. Yet the matter can be politically relevant today; for example, states now wanting to join the European Union have on occasion referred to a cultural inheritance that includes their former membership of medieval Latin Christendom.

There was also to be a further question, first tested in the crusading states set up in the Holy Land in the late eleventh and early twelfth centuries, about the missionary principles to be followed in new colonies established among the infidels, which followed the established Roman Catholic pattern. In Palestine there was, in fact, a great deal of hesitation about trying to convert the Muslims, and in the end nothing resembling a missionary church was established there. In Spain there were many conversions from Islam, but it may be questioned whether the Iberian Christians ever established anything that could be called a missionary church among the conquered Muslims. The question of missionary doctrine and practice in colonies to be established after navigation of the Atlantic and other far-off seas remained in a far-distant future. In the eleventh and twelfth centuries it would have been impossible for people to know that both in Europe and in Palestine they could be setting precedents that would, centuries later, influence the ways in which Christ was brought to very distant, to them unimaginable, lands.

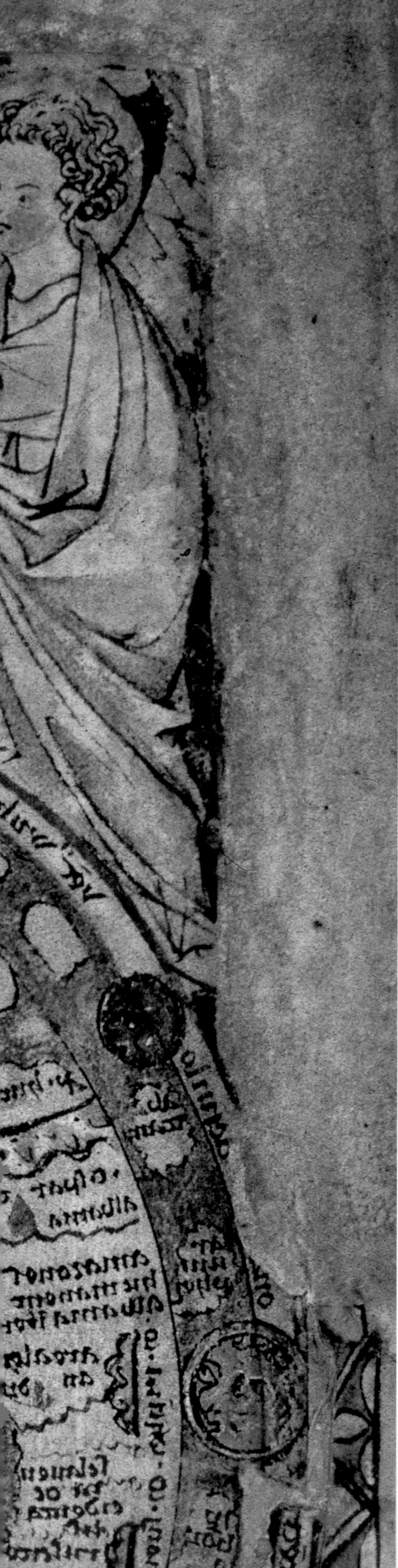

1

MEDIEVAL CHRISTENDOM

How was the preaching of the Christian message to the Gentiles being accomplished, a thousand years after the death of Jesus? Many times, sometimes within the Roman world, sometimes crossing its frontiers, the missionaries had left to fulfil Christ's command: 'Go forth therefore and make all nations my disciples; baptize everywhere in the name of the Father, the Son and the Holy Spirit, and teach them to observe all that I have commanded.' So long as the Roman Empire endured in the form that the human Christ had known it, the command could be kept by following models that went back to apostolic times. But as the ancient Roman Empire disintegrated, new patterns had to be found.

There was in the early medieval Western world a post-apostolic model for the propagation of the Gospel to the heathen; it was that set by Pope Gregory the Great (c.540–604), in the despatch of the Roman mission to the Anglo-Saxons. From the Anglo-Saxon mission field St Augustine of Canterbury sent (as later happened also with the missions of St Boniface in Germany and of the followers of St Methodios in Bulgaria), requests to Rome for law-making decisions about the problems they encountered. The missions were often not able to follow such tidy precedents: the realities of persuading unwilling pagans to give up their way of life were untidy, fragmentary, full of compromise, sometimes marked by the backsliding of the converts and by the martyrdom of the missionaries. But the principle of Roman supervision and control, though not observed in detail, remained intact.

No one speculated in that world about a moral need to distinguish between the preaching of the Gospel message and the imposition of cultural patterns. The biggest moral question occasionally discussed, was whether people should be baptized under the threat of force. But there was also a question, full of meaning for the integrity of cultures, whether the liturgy could be allowed in a language other than Latin. The need to preach in a vernacular the people could understand was not disputed. But the theological dangers of allowing a liturgy to be performed in a barbarian tongue were starkly obvious

Left: A map of the known Christian world at the turn of the first millennium. Jerusalem is at the centre.

Left: In the thirteenth century, Christianity began to regain its power base in Spain, with many conversions from Islam. The story of such a conversion is shown in pictures in the Cantigas de Santa Maria, *a musical narrative of the life of the Virgin made for Alfonso X of León and Castile, known as 'the Wise', who had made important conquests over the Moors of southern Spain.*

In the Western world, the tenth and early eleventh centuries had seen the conversion of the Scandinavian peoples, and of important branches of the Slavs, notably the Poles and the Bohemians. Outside the Slav world, the Hungarians accepted Latin Christianity under King Stephen (d.1038) at the turn of the tenth century. In quite a short time, the Christian Hungarian dynasty was absorbed into the mainstream of Western European politics by marriage alliances that associated it not only with the German royal house, but also with other Christian dynasties, notably with that of the Anglo-Saxons. The resistance of the pagan tribes on the eastern borders of the Holy Roman Empire to Christianization was stiffened by the avid colonialism of the German imperial dynasty. The Wends held out for a long time, and yet further east, the Lithuanians were to remain recalcitrant pagans for another two centuries and more.

Below: Tripoli is captured by the Sultan of Egypt in 1288, from the Tractatum de Septem Vitiis. *The Muslim reconquest of Syria–Palestine marked the end of the Crusader state in the Holy Land.*

To the south-west, the boundaries of Christendom were being extended by the gradual *reconquista* of many of the Islamic lands in Iberia, by the northern Iberian Christian princes. After the death of the last effective successor-ruler to the Iberian 'Umayyad caliphs, 'Abd al-Malik (1008), the Islamic lands in Spain tended to fragment in the hands of minor Muslim warlords, the so-called muluk al-tawa'if or kings of the factions. This enabled the northern Spanish rulers to press steadily southwards into Islamic territories until, after the fall of Toledo in 1085, there was a big military intervention from North Africa by the Almoravid holy-war dynasty of Morocco. This led to the defeat of King Alfonso VI of León-Castile in 1086, and to the re-imposition of a Muslim barrier against Christian reconquest that endured for at least a further twenty years.

Thus, by the time of the fall of Jerusalem to the First Crusade in 1099, the profile of a new Western Christendom could be seen, which in many respects survived for a further three centuries, and lived on in other ways to influence the Europe in which we live today. The religious colonialism that inspired the Crusader state in the Holy Land ended, it is true, with the Muslim reconquest of Syria–Palestine at the end of the thirteenth century, although a kind of Western political expansionism into the eastern Mediterranean persisted through the Middle Ages, and survived into modern times. The pattern of Christian reconquest in Spain led to a rather different solution to the problem of the cohabitation of Islam and Christianity, when the dominant faith became Christian instead of Islamic. For much of the rest of the Middle Ages, the Muslims in the reoccupied areas of the Iberian peninsula were allowed a sort of limited religious freedom, which tapered off towards the end of the period.

The religious framework that held together this whole ramshackle collection of Christian lands in Europe and the Near East in some sense, was the authority of the Roman bishopric, reinforced and reinvigorated by the efforts of the 'Reform' popes of the late eleventh and early twelfth centuries. It was an authority destined to grow in a spectacular manner. The papacy was to become an entirely different organization from the dignified, but in material terms very modest, bishopric that had protected and provided for the pilgrims who came to pray at the sacred Roman sanctuaries, and that had financed itself from modest contributions of 'Peter's Pence' from a few northern countries.

Papacy and Empire

At this period of the high Middle Ages the Christian countries of north-west Europe were on the edge of a great cultural, demographic and economic movement that was to transform their strength in the Mediterranean and western Atlantic lands, as well as in central continental Europe. At this critical moment of Western European development, the papacy was destined to play a key part not only in the religious but also in the political leadership of Western Christendom. Its role could in the latter respect perhaps be said to have been, if looked at over a long period, roughly comparable with that of the secretariat of the United Nations.

How did these things come about? The key lay in the persistent, obstinate assertion by the Roman bishops, over a period of many centuries, of claims to authority and jurisdiction over all the other churches. The critical political element was the integral link between the 'Roman Empire', which had been reinvented for Charlemagne in 800, and the Roman bishops who had the exclusive privilege of crowning the 'emperor'. That for a long time the 'Reform' popes of the high Middle Ages were hostile to the German emperors made no difference to the symbiotic relationship that existed between the two institutions.

But the Crusades represented a new, independent political venture on a European and extra-European scale by the papacy, in whose establishment the Empire had played no part. The principle behind the Crusades, of a papacy with supra-tribal, quasi-military powers, lost no time in influencing events with the Empire. That the lords of the Saxon marches, and the Hohenstaufen German kings behind them, should have turned to the popes in the mid-twelfth century for authority to launch a Crusade against the Wends on their borders, while at the same time a new Crusade against the Muslims was approved by the popes for the Castilian king in Spain, showed the emergence of an ideologically changed Europe.

The Holy Roman Empire, subject to German dynasties and ceremonially connected with the popes, was the other important link in the chain that tied 'Christendom' together. The territorial extent of the Empire, great as it was, was never vast enough to correspond even remotely with the lands of Christendom. The Empire was, however, especially important for the recognition it usually managed to obtain from the Slav lands in the east, as well as from some non-Slavs such as the Hungarians. Its advocates were not shy about vaunting the power of the Holy Roman Empire. The German courtier-bishop, Otto of Freising (?1111–58), wrote a *History of Two Cities* (i.e. the City of God and the Earthly City) that was in effect a world history brought down to his own times. As he was the uncle of the Holy Roman Emperor Frederick I, his comments on the politics of the time are especially valuable. He observed in the mid-twelfth century that the Roman Empire, in so far as it assumed the form of the Greek (i.e. Byzantine) Empire, was a mere shadow of former greatness. 'From Rome power passed to the Greeks, from the Greeks to the Franks, from the Franks to the

Below: Otto of Freising, the German bishop and historian, was a significant enough figure in his own time to be featured in a stained-glass window at the church at Heiligenkreuz (Holy Cross) in Lower Austria.

Lombards, from the Lombards back to the Germans (who can also be considered Franks).' In other words, in Otto's eyes the power of ancient Rome no longer had anything to do with Byzantine 'Rome', but with the Holy Roman Empire of the German house of Hohenstaufen.

In the West, the west Frankish kingdom was evolving into the kingdom of 'France', which owed no allegiance to the Holy Roman Empire, and which, after 1066, was linked through Normandy with the English State. The old Middle Kingdom of Burgundy and the lands north and south of it remained in an ambiguous position. The Iberian kingdoms and principates remained in a separate world of frontiersmen on the borders of Mediterranean and Atlantic Islam. The Scandinavian, Scottish and Irish kings and princes dwelt upon other, largely maritime frontiers. 'Europe' is to a modern European just recognizable in this Western Christian conglomerate.

Right: Fifth Italian Expedition of Emperor Frederick I (1174). A thorn in the side of the papacy, the powerful Hohenstaufen Emperor Frederick I (Barbarossa) dominated proceedings at the Papal Imperial Negotiations in Venice.

The Foundation of Cluny

The faith was the unifying factor, not only through the medium of the Roman Church as an organization, but also through other powerful Church movements that penetrated many kingdoms and regions. The reforming Benedictine abbey of Cluny, in Burgundy, founded early in the tenth century and supported by a Roman papacy that in other respects is supposed to have been at that time corrupt, was the most powerful monastic model of the high Middle Ages. The time of the greatest influence and renown of Cluny was in the second half of the eleventh century, when the great church was built, whose battered and reordered remains can still be seen and admired. Cluniac houses were to be found all over Europe, beginning with the big nucleus in all the lands watered by the Rhine from its source to the sea, but stretching east to Bavaria, west to Normandy and the Loire, south-west through Provence and across the Pyrenees to Navarre and Aragon, and south-east to northern and central Italy. Cluniac priories reached England rather later, but were eventually established from Lewes in the South to Pontefract in the North.

Cluny represented an aristocratic model of piety, it is true, but a noble one, which asserted silence, abstinence, and the dignity and beauty of liturgical worship, and particularly of liturgical music. The Cluniacs were less tied to the support and pursuit of learning than earlier Benedictines, perhaps partly because the great social need for the basic texts had for the time been satisfied. A fine sculptured set of capitals that have survived from the choir of the great church of Cluny, show figures representing the eight keys of the plainchant octave.

Above: The Sounds of Music. A twelfth-century capital from the choir at the abbey church of Cluny, one of eight, each showing a key of the plainchant octave.

In these Cluniac monasteries, the descendants of the great Carolingian foundations of the eighth and ninth centuries, medieval monasticism reached its most extravagant manifestation as at once a refuge from the world, and as the holy pattern put forth for the world to admire. Huge foundations, like Cluny itself, such as Fleury on the Loire, Gorze in Lorraine, Lorsch, St Gallen, Fulda further to the east, were endowed or re-endowed with enormous estates, built or rebuilt on a very big scale, existing as little self-contained, walled clerical towns with all the services a civilized community needed. In areas where all almost all other human habitations were built of wood, they were constructed in stone. The portals of some of these great churches were literally the gates of heaven, decorated on the outside with great sculptural allegories that told the faithful the stories of divine judgement, of prophecy, of salvation.

The Cluniac movement was powerful and effective, but its social objectives were too narrow to continue to fill the needs of a rapidly changing Church. In the twelfth century the Reform Church found a new ideal in a great complex of new monastic houses spreading out – also, like Cluny, from an original base in Burgundy – from the monastery of Cîteaux, the monastic house of the great reforming abbot, St Bernard (1090–1153).

Right: The great tympanum over the west door of the cathedral of St Etienne at Bourges, built 1192–1275, carved in elaborate detail to show exactly what will happen at the Last Judgement. Many worshippers did not read and the graphic use of sculpture and stained-glass imagery helped to convey the Christian message.

Right: St Bernard, co-founder of the Church militant in the form of the Templar Knights, preaches the Second Crusade before the King of France at Vézelay.

On the one hand St Bernard represented the intense activism of the Gregorian reform (so-called after Pope Gregory VII) and its political will to intervene in almost every phase of public life where it saw a moral principle at stake. From that point of view his life is almost a history of the Western European kingdoms of the first four decades of the twelfth century. His correspondence is an address book full of kings, princes, and popes. In the most political of all the Church activities of the time, the Crusade, St Bernard intervened twice in a most decisive way: first he collaborated in the foundation of the first major 'military' order of fighting monks, the Templars, and secondly he played a principal role in the recruitment and organization of the Second Crusade (1146–9), which he launched with a great sermon before the King Louis VII of France and his nobles, in the great church of Vézelay (Yonne), in eastern Burgundy. At this peak point of St Bernard's career, he had been asked by the French king himself to preach the Crusade, and he was so influential that he later managed to persuade the German King Conrad to support it alongside the French.

Above: St Bernard with his demon chained firmly at his side.

Below: The ruins of Rievaulx Abbey, Yorkshire, established in 1131 as the second Cistercian monastery in England.

Cistercian Reform

But from a different point of view St Bernard can be seen as the leader of a great mass movement of penance. He became a great figure in Europe, not from his political fame, but from the immense influence of the monastic reform that he initiated, called 'Cistercian', after the name of the abbey of Cîteaux. The new monasteries founded from Cîteaux swiftly found immense noble and royal support, so that, like the Cluniac houses of two centuries earlier, they grew up all over Europe. More than three hundred had been founded by the time of Bernard's death in 1153. In England their 'bare, ruined choirs' may be seen at Fountains and at Rievaulx in Yorkshire.

The Cistercian movement was based on the desire to praise God and to repent in poverty for sin, in a communal life whose austerity had nothing in common with the liturgical extravagance of the Cluniacs, and which, like the early hermit movements of Eastern Christianity, desired isolation from the world: the public were not admitted to the early Cistercian monasteries. Perhaps, no less than among the Cluniacs of long before, the core members of the Cistercians were penitent noblemen, although, like the Benedictines, the Cistercians did not restrict their recruitment to nobles. Cistercian churches austerely avoided decoration, in the same way as their worship eschewed elaborate music and ritual. Their monastic lives were not so strictly cloistered as those of the Cluniacs, in that they were expected to go outside the monastery into the fields, to work alongside the lay brothers, the conversi. There were economic reasons why this new system worked. Because land had become scarce, Cistercian houses were very often endowed with estates that were only marginally productive, and therefore labour-intensive.

St Bernard was the leader of a great movement of renunciation among the knightly class from which he came. It is not at all surprising that he sponsored the monastic order of Templar Knights, which he saw as another instrument of salvation for the secular knights whose bloodstained lives were otherwise irredeemably condemned by divine judgement. In this way they could continue to give battle, but 'The soldier of Christ kills safely [without peril to his soul]; he dies the more safely. He serves his own interests in dying, and Christ's interests in killing.' Translated into Arabic and given Islamic terminology, these sentiments would be perfectly understood today by the soldiers of Hizbullah.

One of St Bernard's Cistercian monks became pope in 1145 as Pope Eugenius III (pope 1145–53),

Above: A thirteenth-century French bronze sculpture of an armoured knight on horseback. Christian knights could claim salvation, and any killing they had done be forgiven, if they went to war in the name of Christ.

and he issued the papal summons to the Crusade in the following year, after which St Bernard himself preached it at Vézelay. It was a time when the language and concepts of military feudalism had to some extent taken over the Church. To Bernard and his pupil Pope Eugenius, the infidel had stolen the 'patrimony of the crucified one'. As Bernard put it: 'The earth has been shaken: it trembles because the lord of Heaven has begun to lose his land – the land in which, for more than thirty years, he lived as a man among men.' The soldiers, the men of war, could fight in this cause without endangering their souls. The indulgence for sin that followed the taking of the cross to become a fighter for Christ, Bernard represented – ironically, it is true, when he addressed his audience at this point as 'merchants' – as being a splendid bargain, and a great opportunity.

Preaching ideally required good learning as well as godliness. By the sixth century the language of the Western Church had become Latin. Its message could survive without a knowledge of the Greek in which its creeds had originally been formulated, but by this time it was working and preaching in the midst of a babel of barbarian vernacular tongues. For a very long period, from the sixth century until the twelfth, there was no social system in Western Europe that trained fully literate cadres in the way they had been trained in the late Roman Empire. Able, articulate, learned churchmen existed, who very occasionally had some knowledge of Greek as well as of Latin, but their numbers were small. A competent standard of literacy in the Latin tongue could be acquired only in major monasteries, or in certain cathedral schools, or in certain nurseries of courtier-priests attached to royal courts.

The Scholar Class

When in the early twelfth century a growing number of clever young people sought training in rhetoric and philosophy in the schools of north-west France, and particularly in Paris, the consequences were to be important, firstly to the Church, but afterwards to secular society. A member of this intellectually and socially ambitious new class was the thrusting and innovative scholar, Peter Abelard (1079–1142). Having trained himself in logic and debate in the schools of Paris in the first years of the twelfth century, Abelard later extended his studies to theology, and began to teach a rigorous logical method that was applied to divine subjects as well as to philosophy. His book *Sic et non* began: 'Here begin sentences from the holy scriptures which seem opposed to each other...' Abelard's dialectic method did not commend itself to St Bernard, nor, no doubt, did reports of his love affair with Héloïse, who ended as abbess of the nunnery of the community of the Paraclete that Abelard had set up in Champagne. A confrontation with St Bernard in 1140 ended badly for Abelard, who was condemned in Rome, and ended his life two years later as a monk in Cluny.

No such scholarly class as Abelard represented had existed in the Western world since the decay of the Roman Empire. Abelard was predominantly a logician, but as the twelfth century advanced, increasingly such people sought knowledge of Roman law, which was particularly important in the schools of northern Italy, and especially in Bologna. The revival of Roman law was to be very useful to government; immediately it was most useful to Church government. At the end of the Middle Ages, the revival of Roman law was to be one of the main engines behind the creation of the early modern state.

Twelfth-Century Renaissance

Knowledge of Greek began to creep back, although to a very limited extent that was, paradoxically, checked by the organization, in the early thirteenth century, of corporate teaching bodies which turned

Left: Diligent students study logic in a French school. From the twelfth century onwards, there was a growth in secular learning and universities were established all over Europe.

Below: The fourteenth-century statutes of the College of Hubant or the Blessed Virgin, Paris, graphically displayed by its students.

Above: The blighted lovers Abelard and Héloïse, illustrated in the fourteenth-century Le Roman de la Rose, *a French allegorical romance by Guillaume de Lorris and Jean de Meung, and the classic textual expression of the concept of courtly love.*

into 'universities'. The medieval universities developed no satisfactory way of dealing with Greek culture, either in its pagan form, or in its manifestation in the writings of the Greek 'fathers of the Church'. Many of the rediscovered Greek texts, especially those relating to science and philosophy, had been first translated into Arabic, and thence to Latin. The eastern Crusades, however, played little part in encouraging this sort of cultural linkage. Arabo-Greek texts usually reached the West either from importation through the semi-Arabized Norman kingdom of Sicily, or through the Christian kingdoms in Spain.

However, the gains of what has become known as the twelfth-century Renaissance were substantial, both in an intellectual way, and through the social gains of the creation of a new learned class. By the end of the eleventh century a new corpus of knowledge was available, which included quite a large part of the recovered culture of the late Latin Roman world, as well as additional knowledge and speculation that had come from the Arabs. It has been said that one of the great aims of the new intellectual movement was to achieve definitions and to specify boundaries and functions, and that one of the results of such a movement was to exclude whole categories of things and people from the privileged areas of society. This is arguable, although it can also be said that scholastic method enabled people to recognize the legitimacy of diversity. Whether increasingly excluded categories included those of women and homosexuals is a question much discussed, although still not answered.

The Second Crusade, summoned as a result of the Christian loss of the great Syrian fortress of Edessa in 1144, was one of the great medieval examples of international thinking in the politically (or rather, religiously) correct terms of the times. The great medieval rulers, most notably Louis VII of France and – after some hesitation – Emperor Conrad of Germany, embraced the project as mentioned above, and the armies started to march to the East in 1147. Not altogether surprisingly, the whole enterprise ran into political difficulties that rendered it a military failure. European military co-operation on the grand scale has never been easy, and in this case it suffered the more because the relief forces had not put too much effort into finding out what the Christian kingdom of Jerusalem actually wanted or needed. When the two Western sovereigns reached Palestine in 1148, their forces were not strong enough to launch the enterprise in northern Syria that the situation really required. Instead they launched an attack on Damascus, a city ruled by the one Muslim power that was reasonably well disposed towards the Christians. The affair reached a humiliating military conclusion, entirely useless to the Christian cause.

In the long history of the relations between Western and Eastern Christianity, the Second Crusade played a negative part. Its failure was somewhat implausibly blamed upon the Byzantine Empire by some westerners, and no less an authority than St Bernard is thought, towards the end of his life, to have recommended an attack on Byzantium as a preliminary to resuming the attack on Islam. Perhaps others felt as he did, but no action in this direction was to be taken until half a century after St Bernard's death.

The disastrous defeat of the Christian kingdom of Jerusalem at the Battle of Hattin in 1187 was immediately followed by the loss of Jerusalem to the great Muslim leader, Saladin. These traumatic events produced a sharp reaction in the West, which led to the summoning of a new crusading relief force.

The Third Crusade is often seen as the romantic Crusade *par excellence*, and it was certainly seen in this light by Sir Walter Scott when he wrote *Ivanhoe*. But in many respects it was the least sentimental of the earlier Crusades, and was conducted in a spirit of harsh political realism. King

Above: An illustration of the Council of the Kings at Acre from The Council of Acre and the Siege of Damascus *by William of Tyre. The Siege of Acre was a pivotal event in the Second Crusade.*

Philip Augustus of France and his vassal, King Richard of England, who accepted the challenge on behalf of the feudal West, were a great deal more able in both a political and a military sense, than had been the leaders of the Second Crusade. The Third Crusade began in Palestine in 1191, and the fall of Acre to the Christians in the same year was a severe blow to Saladin.

The victory of Acre was achieved by Christian leaders who no longer seriously thought of total

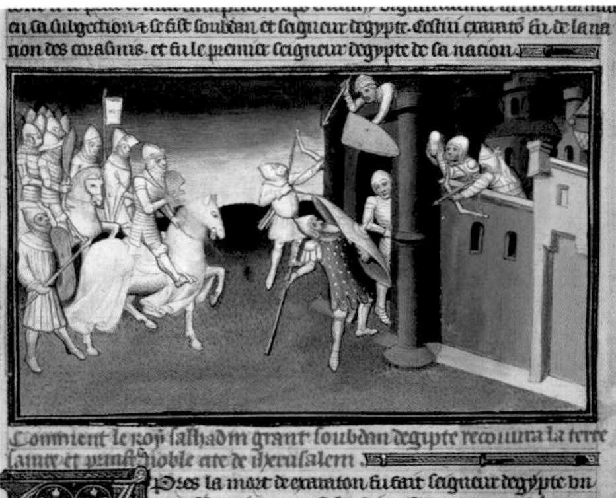

Above: The Saracen leader Saladin captures Jerusalem in 1187.

Left: King Richard I of England tilting at Saladin. From the Luttrell Psalter (prior to 1340).

victory in the East, and who, although they often used the language of passionate committment to holy war, recognized that the recapture of Jerusalem was probably unattainable. When they withdrew, it was under a system of truces with the Ayubid successors of which Saladin, was to serve more or less as a model for the Christian political presence in Palestine as long as it endured.

In people's minds the Crusade dwelt on that boundary between power politics and fantasy that is one of the most treacherous and dangerous zones of human consciousness. Because the Jerusalem envisaged in Christian imagery was not a real city, but one whose bulwarks were strong with salvation, and whose streets were of shining gold, the humble details of Palestinian politics were – as they almost certainly still are – irrelevant to what was thought about the city. Nothing could eliminate Jerusalem from Christian imagination. The recapture of Jerusalem by the Christians was something that, three centuries later, Christopher Columbus thought might be accomplished by his voyages: in that kind of perspective, local truces made by Crusaders with Muslim emirs do not loom very large. Concretely, if the crusading state was to survive at all in Palestine, it had to do so through a system of diplomatic deals with the local Arab rulers, and that was the way in which the Crusaders managed

Right: A pilgrim contemplates an abandoned suit of armour on the road to Jerusalem. The dream of recapturing the city for eternal Christendom was never fulfilled.

to remain in an ever-shrinking Christian enclave, almost until the end of the thirteenth century. But

Left: Jerusalem, from the Book of Hours *of Duke René of Anjou (1409–80). René claimed the thrones of both Naples and Jerusalem, although he occupied neither.*

SECVRI TAS
SENÇ
ELAVO
MEN
MANT
CHEL

© AKG London/Erich Lessing

2

Popes, Cathedrals and Crusades

Behind the revival of learning and the building of the great cathedrals and castles in north-west Europe lay the economic and demographic revival that enabled medieval society to pay for them. The twelfth century had been the great age of forest clearance ('assarts' as the English called them), which added huge areas of arable land and pasture everywhere between lowland Scotland and eastern Germany, and that led, also, to the more intensive exploitation of the now-destroyed, but in its day immensely important, resource of the forest. On the back of increased agricultural production, population climbed. In northern and coastal Italy, northern France, England and Flanders, the towns expanded their economic and commercial activities, perhaps modestly in single instances, but collectively, an advance was made on a huge scale.

Everywhere kings, nobles and bishops supported the foundation of urban-style settlements, often at first small, in order to tax them to finance their own lifestyles and their warfare. The burgess, or burgher, or bourgeois, became an important economic and social factor. Great new centres of mercantile and monetary exchange, markets and 'fairs', came into existence in areas such as Champagne. The art of war attracted big investments in skilled warriors and their mounts, in better equipment, in improved fortifications. Crusading lords learned new techniques of fortification in Syria, and returned to build great castles in Normandy, England and elsewhere that set entirely new

© Bibliothèque Nationale, Paris, France/Bridgeman Art Library

Above: As administration costs rose, more taxes were levied.

Left: Detail from the fresco entitled Allegory of Good Government *by Ambrogio Lorenzetti (Palazzo Pubblico, Siena), illustrating a well-run and thriving town, protected by stout walls and served by neatly kept fields and farms. At this time, towns began to expand their economic and commercial activities.*

Above: A battle scene on a town wall in Syria. Many of the taxes raised paid for armaments and military techniques copied from the Syrian example.

standards of siege warfare. The castles constructed by Henry II (1139–89) and Richard I of England, particularly, in the valleys of the Loire and the Seine, were vast, expensive war machines of a kind never seen before in Europe. The seas were ploughed by new mercantile routes, and carried new bulk trades such as those in dried fish and wine; inland, new trading routes across Germany and the Alps opened great markets for salt, for textiles, for weapons.

In northern Italy especially, the urban settlements acquired their own style of government and an independence that was at first circumscribed. However, by the late twelfth century the 'communes' of northern and central Italy had outgrown a lot of the irksome controls and taxes imposed on them by bishops and German emperors, and organized themselves into groups such as the 'Lombard League', which possessed real military and political clout. The maritime Italian cities, especially Genoa, Pisa and Venice, profited from the general revival of trade, and from specific privileges in Eastern commerce that their stake in the crusading kingdom in Palestine gave them, to gain European political importance. Small colonial trading counters of this kind were the model for much of the later penetration of the Italian merchants into the eastern Mediterranean.

Left: The remains of a Crusader castle at Byblos, in the Lebanon. Such castles were considered state-of-the-art fortifications and inspired castle design in England, for example.

Below: Henry II built many chateaux in France, particularly along the Loire. This is the castle at Saumur, illustrating the month of September in the Très Riches Heures of the Duc de Berry.

In this great economic and cultural movement the Church played a leading part, because of its existing wealth and power, and control of scarce investment resources, because of its enormous advantages in disposing of very scarce trained personnel, and perhaps most of all because it controlled most of the main channels of cultural advance.

The Great Churches

However, the clergy could not exclude the laity from profiting from social developments that looked clerical, but were not always entirely so in their results. Huge social investments were made in great churches and monasteries, whose functions were not only to proclaim and teach the faith, but also to propagate the images of the power and religious zeal of the noble families, and even more of the new monarchies. Through church coronations and crown-wearing ceremonies, in which the kings were in effect worshipped by their subjects, the Church legitimized and honoured the monarchs who were in many respects its rivals. In England for example, the great cathedrals particularly linked with the crown were those at Westminster, Winchester and Gloucester, all places where William the

Below: The interior of Durham Cathedral, the masterpiece of Romanesque architecture that symbolized the Norman power in England in the twelfth and thirteenth centuries.

Conqueror had worn his crown on the great feasts. The huge cathedrals of Durham and York had also been symbolic of Norman power, in the earlier years of the Norman conquest, and they remained symbolic of royal power in the north at least until the time of Queen Elizabeth I.

The clergy, who were directly responsible for commissioning and financing the great churches, built them to serve the demands of the holy liturgy, and to provide an architectural setting for it which responded to the very practical requirements of the holy ceremonies and their adjuncts (such as saints' shrines), and also in its own language of stone, offered a worthy praise to God. The programmes of church decoration, including those of the new art of the stained-glass windows, were also huge manifestations of the elaborate symbolism that underlaid all sacramental Catholicism: this had aspects that were not only directly symbolic, such as the great visions of heaven and hell in the sculpture of the cathedral portals, but also mathematical, produced by a sort of science of holy numbers. The revival of learning and the changes in theological emphasis in the twelfth century had direct results on the decorative programmes, so that the great visions of Christ the Judge that inspired the earlier cathedrals were later changed to envisage a Christ who was the object of tender adoration by his human mother.

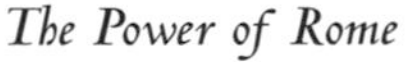

The Power of Rome

At the heart of the clerical transformations of the twelfth and thirteenth centuries lay the Roman bishopric, the papacy. The whole thrust of the Gregorian Reform movement, of the struggle against simony, of the foundation of new monastic orders and their authorization, of the astonishing innovation of the Crusade and the Christian settlement in the Holy Land, came from Rome. The Roman Court, which before 1046 had been run by a little-known group of Roman clerks, had by the late twelfth century become an elite European institution, which drew for its personnel on all the main feudal kingdoms of Europe, but especially upon the Holy Roman Empire, upon the French monarchy, and occasionally upon England.

The inevitable result of giving place in a court to any kin group, whether that court was lay or clerical, was that other members of the kinship and the region from which it came followed them to court preferment. When the Englishman, Robert Pullen, a former Oxford lecturer on theology, was made Papal Chancellor in 1144 he used his influence to prefer several Englishmen to office in the papal court. One, Nicholas Breakspear, became pope ten years later as Hadrian IV (pope 1154–9), the only English pope ever to be chosen. As pope, he organized a further development of the papal state as a feudal organization with the military power that it needed to protect the

Left: The stunning rose window in the north transept of Chartres Cathedral. The Virgin and Child are in the centre encircled by figures from the Old Testament. The decoration of churches was at once a way to praise God and an educational device for the illiterate. Stained-glass production was at the time the cutting edge of technology.

Above: A posthumous engraving of Hadrian IV, the only Englishman (so far) to become pope.

Right: The royal seal of Henry II – a Norman king in full Norman armour.

pilgrim roads to Rome; to do this he used techniques he had learned in the centralized feudal society of contemporary England. He also had to cope with Arnold of Brescia (c. 1100–55), an anti-clerical preacher who had been welcomed by the Romans in order to give some ideological colour to their attempt to assert independence from their bishop, the pope, on the north Italian 'communal' model. Hadrian, with a brusqueness of which Henry II of England must have been proud, had Arnold executed. Pope Hadrian also obliged Henry by recognizing his lordship of Ireland.

The cardinals in Rome, were in principle the priests of the main Roman churches and the heads of the various diaconates that had carried out charitable functions in Rome. Together with the bishops of a few churches located just outside Rome, they became the chief figures of a new papal civil service, and the privileged principals of a new clerical aristocracy, which elected the bishop of Rome, the pope.

The papacy was far bigger than any of its servants. Its position rested above all on scripture, and the twelfth and thirteenth centuries were the golden age of scriptural interpretation in an allegorical sense, in which the holy writings could be used as a topical basis for conferring authority on certain privileged clergy in modern situations. The power conferred upon Peter by Jesus to bind and to loose both on earth and in heaven (Matt. 16: 19–20) was the basic text, that may today be seen girding the interior of the great dome of St Peter's in Rome. But scripture as a whole was deemed to stand behind the bishops who succeeded Peter at Rome. Pope Innocent I (401–17) had addressed a letter to the bishop of Rouen, according to which any major church lawsuit ought to be referred for decision to the Roman bishop. Pope Innocent alleged as his reason that in the Bible Moses was advised by God to set up judge over the people (Exodus 18:22), but to reserve great matters for himself. In the words of a great and trenchant scholar:

'The standpoint marked the beginning of the Bible as a pièce justicative *of papal governmental pronouncements. In crucial matters, papal principles were not to rest on tradition, history, synodal statutes or other man-made organs. Among all historically evolved governments this was a unique phenomenon. Reality was to be subject to the ideology enshrined in the law, and in its basic ingredients this ideology was the sum-total of the Christian faith... For the internal substance of the papal law was said to be biblically inspired and derived. This is the same as saying that the papacy interpreted and applied the divine law of the Bible to the exigencies of the government of the Christian body itself.'*

Walter Ullman did not write this in order to support a 'Catholic' sectarian view of papal power. On the contrary, he thought that the papal monarchy in the sense of these words had ceased to exist by the end of the Middle Ages, and the verdict was Ullman's historical judgement on medieval Christendom.

Canon Law

If the claims of the Roman See were so all-embracing, to be fully effective they had to be articulated in a rational and systematic way. This was part of the meaning of the renaissance of legal studies in the twelfth century. A scholar, or perhaps more than one legal scholar, whose name has come down to us as Gratian, produced, probably in Bologna in the early 1140s, a work called the *Concord of Discordant Canons,* or the reconciliation of conflicts between Church laws. Its logical method was in many ways similar to that of Abelard's *Sic et Non* of the preceding period, which had drawn the thunders of St Bernard upon its author. However, Gratian's work was not to have the effect of disintegrating faith in Church law, but, on the contrary, of enhancing the juristic supremacy of the Roman See, of which St Bernard so much approved.

Gratian's work was to become the foundation of later medieval canon law, which amounted to a system for running the whole huge structure of the Western Church on an increasingly centralized basis, based on Roman law principles, and supervised by courts that were either located in Rome, or set up under papal mandate. Not all canonists in the Middle Ages fully accepted the maximum claims that were made for papal power, but enough support for the high view of papal supremacy existed to make it very important in Western legal culture. These tendencies had already existed before Gratian, and St Bernard wrote a work, entitled *De Consideratione,* that tried to advise his protégé, who had become pope as Pope Eugenius III, on how to preserve spiritual values when the papal institution over which he presided was effectively an overworked law court, almost continuously in session. Far from declining, and so giving the popes more room to consider spiritual matters, as Bernard had hoped, the work of the Roman bishopric as the highest Christian court overwhelmingly increased. All clerical Europe turned to Rome to ask its courts to do justice, so making the papacy into a new and different institution.

Right: Pope Innocent III, who came to office as a young man, shown in papal regalia on a fresco in the monastery of St Benedict in Subiaco (the 'Sacro Speco').

PP. III.
INNO
EPS SERVVS SERVORV DI. DILECTIS FILI PRIORI ET FRIB IVXTA
NEDICTI REGLARE VITA SERVANTIBVS IN INTER HOLOCAVSTA
MAGIS EST MEDVLLATV QVA OFFERTVR ALTISSIMO DE PINGVEDINE
IT ATTENDENTES. CV OLI CAVSA DEVOTIONIS ACCESSISSEM AD LOCV
NEDICT SVE CONVERSIONIS PRIMORDIO CONSECRAVIT. ET IVENISSEM VOS IBI
VS LAVDABILITER DNO FAMVLANTES. NE PROTEPORALIS SVBSTENTATIONIS
VANTIE DISCIPLINA TORPERET. APOSTOLICV VOBIS SVBSIDIV

A Young Pope

Under these changing circumstances a young nobleman from the Roman countryside was elected pope in 1198 as Pope Innocent III. He was less than thirty years old when he became pope. He was already a cardinal, and the author of a treatise, *On the Misery of the Human Condition*, a subject that failed to announce that his pontificate was going to be marked by ruthless political activism. He had been accounted an 'Abraham of theology', and was also a distinguished jurist. His tenure of the Roman See (1198–1216), occurred at a critical moment in European history, and his ability and decisiveness were to prove critical in moulding the later medieval papacy.

For the forty years preceding the pontificate of Innocent III, central Italy, and the papacy with it, had been dominated by the aggressive Swabian-German dynasty of Hohenstaufen. The Italian lands of the popes had been treated as part of the Holy Roman Empire, and the popes had found it very difficult to escape Hohenstaufen political influence. But in 1197 the premature death of the Hohenstaufen Emperor Henry VI, who had been a powerful German ruler, and in Italy had ruled as far south as Sicily, gave Innocent the political opportunities he needed to free the papacy from imperial tutelage for ever. The old school of nationalist German historians judged the early death of Henry VI and its subsequent political exploitation by Innocent III to have been the most terrible disaster of medieval German history, whose consequences blocked the creation of a German national state in roughly the same period as the national states of France, England, or Spain were being formed.

Below: The imperial seal of Otto IV, the unsuccessful Saxon claimant to the Holy Roman crown.

The Struggle for Empire

Innocent III claimed to be the feudal lord and protector in the southern Italian kingdom of Sicily, of Henry VI's son, the infant Frederick II, and he claimed also to be a kind of supreme judge and arbitrator, when a disputed succession to the German kingdom and the Holy Roman Empire occurred after Henry's death. The contrasting claimants to the Empire were Philip of Swabia, the Hohenstaufen, brother of the dead emperor, and Otto IV of Saxony (c.1174–1218), son of the great ruler of the eastern German marches, Henry the Lion. There was no agreed protocol for election to the Empire, which did not fall to the successor by simple right of birth. It was widely felt that the election belonged to a 'College' of German electoral princes. The rights to the Empire of the infant papal ward, Frederick II, were also canvassed.

The uncertain situation of the Empire enabled Innocent III to seek papal political advantage. By subtle manoeuvre he represented the quarrel as one that had been referred to his court for decision. In 1200 he issued a papal 'Deliberation' that came down on the side of the Saxon Otto, and against the Hohenstaufen princes who had in the past proved unfavourable to the Holy See. Innocent did not make crude claims of supremacy over temporal rulers, but he claimed powers to intervene in their affairs in cases that involved moral or religious lapses, or when they had actually appealed to his court for decision.

The long and complex story of Innocent III's involvement in the struggle for the Empire once or twice seemed about to end in misfortune for the papacy, especially when, after Innocent's break with Otto IV, Otto's armies seemed set in 1211 to control both the kingdom of Sicily and the papal state. Innocent III riposted by supporting young Frederick II's claims to the Empire, and, after Otto IV and his English allies had been decisively defeated by France at the Battle of Bouvines in 1214, the papal gambit met with success. Innocent had played for high stakes, and won.

The Betrayal of the Eastern Church?

A not dissimilar story of risky but successful political opportunism on the part of Innocent III was played out in the matter of the Crusade, the organization of which he was in theory responsible for. It was during the Fourth Crusade that the differences between the ideals and the reality of the Crusade came to tragic prominence. The stumbling block was the hiring of sea transport to take the armies to fight the Muslims. Under papal leadership and guidance crusading armies had been assembled in Western Europe in 1202 to fight in the East, most probably in Egypt, although Palestine was still a possibility. But the only possible carriers for the crusading armies were the fleets of the maritime republic of Venice, and money to hire their ships was not available. The only way to buy Venetian compliance was to accept their required change to the proposed route of the Crusaders, which was diverted, first to expel the Hungarians from Zara on the eastern coast of the Adriatic Sea, in pursuit of Venetian political aims, and then to sail to Constantinople. Neither had ever figured in the original programme of the Crusaders.

In Constantinople in 1204 both the Venetians and the crusading leaders had their own agenda to execute. Internal conflicts of Byzantine politics enabled the crusading force, with Venetian encouragement, to chase away the legitimate Eastern Emperor, Alexius III, and to establish its own candidate, the Emperor's nephew (also called Alexius). The Western puppet ruler, the young Alexius IV, was subsequently driven from the throne by a revolt and murdered, but the crusading armies refused to accept the ruler, the even shorter-lived Alexius V, who replaced him. In pursuance of supposedly legitimate claims, the Crusaders attacked and stormed Constantinople.

Below left. The sign of the Venetian Boat Builders' Guild. Venice controlled a seller's market supplying ships to ferry crusading armies to their destination.

Below: Frederick II on the throne of the Holy Roman Empire, which he gained with the support of Pope Innocent III.

Above: Crusading continued after Innocent III's time but was not much more successful. The knights of the Seventh Crusade (1248–54), led by Louis IX of France, took Damietta in Egypt but were captured by Turks and held to very expensive ransom.

After eight hundred years of sporadic barbarian attacks on East Rome, and as many years of bickering and quarrels between Eastern and Western Churches, the eventual decision had come as a result of a sordid bargain about ship-chartering. The sack of what was still incomparably the richest and most civilized city in the Christian world took three loot-crammed days. Not only was treasure and plunder of every conceivable sort stuffed into so-called crusading hands, but also the greatest collection of Christian relics in the world was seized with equal cupidity, for presentation or sale to the Western Church.

The absent and theoretical master of the Fourth Crusade was Pope Innocent III, who had formally forbidden an attack on Constantinople, although his earlier involvement with the Byzantine prince, Alexius, gave colour to some of the manoeuvres of the Crusaders. In his dealings with the Eastern Church he showed an inflexible and insensitive front. He gave only dusty, autocratic, legalistic answers to the spiritual problems that had accumulated between the two Churches over a period of many centuries. To the equally long history of political problems, Innocent offered the answer of armed force.

When Constantinople fell, the pope accepted the *fait accompli*, and approved the 'Latin Empire' that was set up under Baldwin of Flanders (1171–1206), albeit after a division of the spoils, made before the attack on the city, which left a sizeable slice to the Venetians. In the event, the Western adventurers managed to establish a durable Latin occupation of large parts of Greece, notably the Morea, Achaea, Epirus, Athens, and Negroponte that the Venetians had seized. But they lacked the political and military ability to hold on to anything closely resembling the former Empire of Constantinople. Constantinople became the centre of an Eastern Latin 'Empire'. But the Frankish hold on the once-great city was weak, and it is surprising that Frankish rulers held on to Constantinople as late as 1261, when the Greek Empire of Nicaea finally expelled them. Orthodox emperors once more ruled in Constantinople from 1261 until the Ottoman Turks closed the whole chapter by their capture of the city for Islam in 1453.

When he tried to sum up the new situation that had emerged after the fall of Constantinople in 1204, Innocent III wrote that the Greek Church had sailed in a ship that had caught nothing, but that the Roman Church had caught a great shoal of fish [Luke 5:5]. The Greeks had rashly dared to separate themselves from the unity of the universal Church, but now they had returned to the obedience of the Apostolic See like a daughter to a mother – or so Innocent thought. It was a strange way of referring to the sack of a great city and the attempted conquest of an Empire; it looked more like rape than like motherly love. It was an example of St Augustine's principle of 'compel them to come in', applied to a large part of the ancient Church of the East. In this way Innocent III purported to allow a feat of arms by self-interested merchants and soldiers to decide the issue of Christian unity.

Centralization and Dissent

During Innocent III's lifetime most of the big issues that were to preoccupy the Western Church for the following two or three centuries came to light, and so did many of the ways in which orthodox Catholicism was to react to them. It was a measure of the speed at which the organization of the Church had been centralized under Roman leadership, that Innocent himself became aware of the problems, and decided, in many cases, the policies by which he hoped the Church could deal with them. The degree of effective central Church organization at that time should not be exaggerated: poor communications, and the obstinate independence of medieval churches and churchmen, who were supported by a great body of legal custom and by the stout regionalism of their lay constituents, meant that papal bureaucracy and jurisdiction remained, very often, only a thin covering imposed over a chaotic and diverse reality.

When we say that one of the great problems of the Church at the turn of the twelfth century was that of dissent, we must beware of attributing to medieval society a sort of monolithic ideological unity that actually belongs to authoritarian industrial cultures, and not to pre-industrial agricultural ones. It is true that heretics were seen in the Middle Ages by ordinary Christians as demonic adversaries who ought to be savagely treated. For example, Henry II of England, who deferred to no one as an advocate of fierce central power, enacted that wandering heretics ought to be 'presented' by local juries and punished. Yet on the other hand, a lot of freedom of expression

Above: Heretics got short shrift and were lucky if mere expulsion was their lot. Here Albigensians (southern variants of the Cathars) are driven naked from Cerlesonne.

Below: Thomas Aquinas, the great Dominican theologian and philosopher. In his youth he had been known as 'the Dumb Ox' but later his intellect was to shape medieval Europe.

was available to medieval scholars and clerks, both as to their opinions and to their actions. Abelard's chequered career speaks both for the freedom that such clerks could have, and for the hazards they ran from official repression. The biggest ideological dangers, however, were deemed to be those presented by wandering strangers who proselytized for false religions.

Cathars and Dominicans

There were perhaps some historic links between medieval Catharism – the word came from the Greek word meaning 'pure' – and the Manichaeism of the late Roman Empire, but the Cathar movement of religious dissent that came to the surface in early twelfth-century France and Germany was related to religious currents in the contemporary Balkans. In it there was an underlying religious dualism that saw the universe as disputed by two opposed principles of good and evil. Like some of the earlier Gnostics, the Cathars thought that full religious enlightenment was granted to a superior class of 'perfect' believers, who were sexually chaste vegetarians in their way of life, and that a minor degree of enlightenment and a less severe regime could be allowed to the more numerous 'hearers' of the religion. For both 'perfects' and 'hearers' the supreme rite of religion was the 'consolamentum', a form of final initiation that the perfect received on being admitted to their order, and that the hearers received only on their deathbeds. The Cathars, because of their dualism, denied the sacramentalism of orthodox Catholicism, and rejected Catholic principles of Church order. They nevertheless retained a class of 'bishops', leaders who were recruited from their perfect members. They denounced the Christian holy war, and some of them rejected the idea of capital punishment.

Preaching campaigns had been conducted in the south of France, where the Cathars were especially strong, by earlier church leaders, including St Bernard, but Innocent III with typical militaristic zeal resolved on more forceful methods of persuasion. After the murder of a papal legate sent to the area, in 1209 Innocent adapted the precedent of the crusading armies sent to the East to fight for the faith, and had a Crusade preached against the Cathar heretics of Languedoc. It was a fateful decision, because it modified the whole concept of the Crusade, and became the model for many subsequent Crusades that in the later Middle Ages were to be preached against Christian dissidents, some because they were deemed heretics, others because they had offered political opposition to papal policies. The Cathar Crusade of 1209 resulted in the massacre of the population of Béziers, and the expulsion of whole populations of other areas of Languedoc from their homes, including that of the city of Carcassone.

Fighting the Cathar heresy also led to a further innovation, that of the setting up of a new order of travelling preachers, in a religious organization that had secured papal approval. Initially the preaching friars entrusted with these duties were the followers of a Spanish canon called Dominic of Caleruega (c.1170–1221), who initiated a policy of giving his friars a thorough theological training in the schools of Paris and Bologna. To these 'Dominicans' was committed the double duty of preaching the orthodox faith in areas where heresy was rife, and of acting as a religious police force to seek out and punish heresy, sometimes invoking the help of the lay power to impose the death penalty (by burning) upon the most serious offenders. Employing friars of this kind to preach without asking the permission of local bishops to do so was in itself an important act of papal power, which derogated from the authority of the bishops, and emphasized the central element in papal church government.

The policing function of the early friars led to new legal procedures being adopted that were much less favourable to the accused than earlier ones, and that were also the legal precursors for the Inquisition of heresy suspects in forms that lasted into the early modern period. Although their duties were in one way strongly repressive, and drew down on them the appellation of the 'hounds of God', the intellectual integrity of the Dominicans was established early. They acquired a reputation for the disinterested pursuit of intellectual truth; the greatest systematic theologian of the Middle Ages, St Thomas Aquinas (1225–74), was a Dominican.

The friar was a new phenomenon in the life of the Church, in the manner in which he appeared in the early thirteenth century. In another aspect friars were as old as the Church itself, and their wanderings recalled the way in which St Paul and his companions had wandered in Asia Minor and elsewhere to preach and encourage the faith. Dominic had addressed himself to what were comparatively specific problems of the Church of his time, notably the lack of preachers who were properly instructed and trained, and were free of the constraints of either the parish or the older monastic systems.

The Franciscan Way

In central Italy a very different kind of inspired figure appeared who is hard to put into any definite Church category save that of the ascetic hermit holy man, but whose huge imaginative and vital force were to have a profound effect. Francis of Assisi (1181–1226) was a layman, an early thirteenth-century contemporary of Dominic, who underwent a drastic conversion experience that made him become an immensely attractive lay preacher, the organizer of vast campfire missions. His entirely unconventional formulation of his religious experiences, and the way in which he supposed that the words of the Gospels could be followed in a spirit of literal obedience, could easily have led to his indictment and punishment as a heretic.

But the submission of Francis to Church authority, and the extraordinary tolerance and sympathy for his movement displayed by Pope Innocent III, led things in a quite different direction. Francis was a rich merchant's son, and from this aspect he represented a new 'bourgeois' variation upon the ancient theme of the penitent Christian nobleman. The immediacy of his vision, and the way in which it included all natural creation, from the sun to the birds, has made an immense impression from that day to this, especially, in modern times, because his wanderings under the wide skies of Umbria were so memorably recorded by painters working in Umbria, from the time of Giotto onwards.

Within a few years of the death of Innocent III the 'Franciscan' movement had been officially approved by the pope as a new religious order of wandering preachers, living under a vow of obedience and poverty, and under a 'Rule' that still managed to contain some of the poetic and direct moral involvement of its author and founder. The Franciscans were to prove in many

Below: St Dominic shown presiding over the burning of heretics in a painting made by Justus van Gent in the fifteenth century. The Dominicans were often given the right to detain heretics.

Above: A rendering of a dream experienced by Innocent III: Francis of Assisi is shown literally holding up the Lateran Church. The Lateran Council tightened up papal laws.

respects to be a new way in which a Church that, although it became every year more authoritarian and centralized, still managed somehow to reach and appeal to the Christian masses, and to show some concern for the Christian poor.

Lateran Law

In November 1215, Innocent III presided over the Fourth Lateran Council held at the palace of that name in Rome. It was a manifestation of the strength of medieval Latin Christendom. The main bishops of the Eastern churches did not attend, and the Council may not be called 'oecumenical', but bishops came from Eastern and Central Europe, from Bohemia, Hungary, Poland, Livonia and further east. There was diplomatic representation from all the main feudal states of the West and of the crusading East. The Council was attended by more than four hundred bishops and some eight hundred monastic abbots and provosts, and it legislated for the life of the Church on an appropriately grand scale, as well as calling for a new Crusade in the East.

Summing up the work and vision of the great pope, the new Church laws passed by the Lateran Council aimed, in the same spirit as the Reform popes of the previous two centuries, at correcting the lives of the clergy by appropriate disciplinary machinery applied by the bishops. It aimed at extirpating heresy by inquisitorial methods and at tightening up the laws that forbade the clergy to be involved in bloodshed – a rigour that went ill with inquisitorial and crusading policies which at the same time were virtually militarizing the Church.

Above all, the Lateran decrees increased the pastoral responsibilities of the lower clergy and to some extent placed them under indirect central control. For the first time in the history of the medieval Church, every adult in the entire Latin communion was to be obliged to confess his or her sins once a year, to do appropriate penance, and to receive the Eucharistic sacrament at the Easter feast. The enforcement of this canon entailed an enormous educational and disciplinary effort on the part of the clergy, who had never before been set specific pastoral aims in this manner. Tariffs of

Right: A Lateran decree meant that every adult had to confess his or her sins once a year and atone for them. This illustration of Confession is from a more secular source, John Gower's fourteenth-century poem, Confessio Amantis *(The Lover's Confession.)*

penances had often been imposed by local synods in the past, but this enactment conferred an entirely new importance upon private confession, and set a pastoral agenda that was only to be fully implemented in the Catholic Church of the so-called Counter-Reformation of early modern times.

The achievement of Innocent III cannot be summed up in some abstract formula of the attainment of papal centralization, although that was certainly one of his aims. He possessed an extraordinary consciousness of both the political and the social role of the Church, and of its historical and geographical dimension. He may be said, in some ways for the better, in others for the worse, to have defined medieval Christendom, and to have given it its mission.

I W. Ullman, *A Short History of the Papacy in the Middle Ages* (London, 1972), pp. 17-18

Below: Francis of Assisi's new, more humane Order was quickly recognized by Pope Innocent III and ratified his successor.

3

Inquisition, Plague and Schism

Pope Innocent III had made the 'spiritual' power triumph over the material power; in medieval terms he had used the powers both of the spiritual and material swords that Christ had given to Peter. He had brought the moral supervision of the Church home to millions of Christian men and women. In the centuries that followed Innocent III, the Easter feast, with its Good Friday re-enactment of divine sacrifice and restitution, was made into a social fact, described in our own times as part of a 'social miracle', through which, whatever the shortcomings of individuals, salvation was accepted as a social goal.[1] Usurers and drivers of dishonest and oppressive bargains felt obliged, in huge numbers, to make restitution at their deaths for transactions whose morality they doubted. Holy men were appealed to by communities in dispute, and the feuds that tore medieval society to pieces were often settled – although usually only for a time – by such men as Francis of Assisi and his many successors.

Medieval society can easily be sentimentalized. Its personal and communal violence can still be experienced by anyone who attentively opens Chaucer – who was not innocent of using violence in his own private life. But there is still no doubt that the thickening texture of medieval

Above: Geoffrey Chaucer, author of The Canterbury Tales *and chronicler of the bawdier aspects of medieval life.*

Left: Generous offerings from a layman to the clergy in return for intercession with God in the hope of salvation.

Above: The parish church became the centre of rural life.

Below: The rise of capitalism bought wages, taxes and tithes with it.

Church life, with its burgeoning 'fraternities' at local level, and its penetration of so many aspects of the village community, did a great deal to civilize Western Europe. The medieval parishes had plenty about them that was shabby in every sense, it is true. But four centuries later, the Reformation clergy were still dealing with very similar social problems as had occupied the medieval Catholic clergy, and the pastoral agenda of the churches did not change in a fundamental way until the coming of industrial society.

But a big institutional price had to be paid for the top-heavy Church of the later Middle Ages, that in spite of the undoubted moral earnestness of the Reform papacy had not really succeeded in cutting itself free of the ties that bound it to the military elites. Innocent III had, on the contrary, consummated the militarization of the Church, and especially had militarized the papacy itself. The popes became central Italian feudal rulers, with their own military needs. Big military needs meant big cash needs. The most obvious way to allow the popes to have armies was to ask the other bishoprics to pay for them. Within a few years, Pope Gregory IX (pope 1227–41) was calling on the English clergy to give him a tenth of their revenues for his wars. Such payments were fiercely resisted, and it was a further century before the European clergy could be got to pay them in something resembling an organized way. But the process of central clerical taxation had begun.

The churches throughout Europe were still collectively rich, although they were gradually being made to yield to laymen some of the immense lands they had held in the early Middle Ages. Gradually the popes became implacable and efficient tax collectors, who registered in Rome the complex transactions that took place among the European clergy, and compelled them – aided by the slowly growing European credit operations of the Italian banking firms – to pay taxes according to fixed tariffs. There was also a big clerical taxation system attached to the organization of Crusades. The popes raised very large sums indeed to finance crusading projects, and since these projects were to be effected by feudal rulers, the feudal rulers made sure that they secured early access to their crusading funds.

In Rome it did not seem to the popes that they controlled a powerful military machine; on the contrary they felt vulnerable and exposed to aggressive, powerful rulers such the Emperor Frederick II (emperor 1220–50). Frederick was Innocent III's former protégé, later the cultivated ruler of lands stretching from the North Sea to the south Sicilian coasts, and the author of a successful compromise with the Ayubid sultans in the Holy Land that guaranteed Christian access to the holy places of Jerusalem. The papal wars with Frederick II, struggles between papal allies known as 'Guelphs' and imperialist allies known as 'Ghibellines', were bitterly fought all over central and northern Italy.

The struggle with heresy continued under Innocent's successors, as did its growingly systematic suppression by Church tribunals. The Cathars were by no means the only dissenters. There were also Waldensians, Poor Men of Lyons, and other evangelical groups whose main emphasis was placed not on any form of alternative Church hierarchy, but on the action of small groups who supported wandering preachers. The aim, as it was with the Cathars and with the Catholic Church itself, was salvation, but a tragic intolerance, perhaps inevitable in a society that made social action one with religious doctrine, meant that the evangelists were seen by the Inquisitors and the bishops primarily as a problem of policing. They could not see their way to incorporating this evangelical fervour into the Church, as they had managed to do with Francis of Assisi.

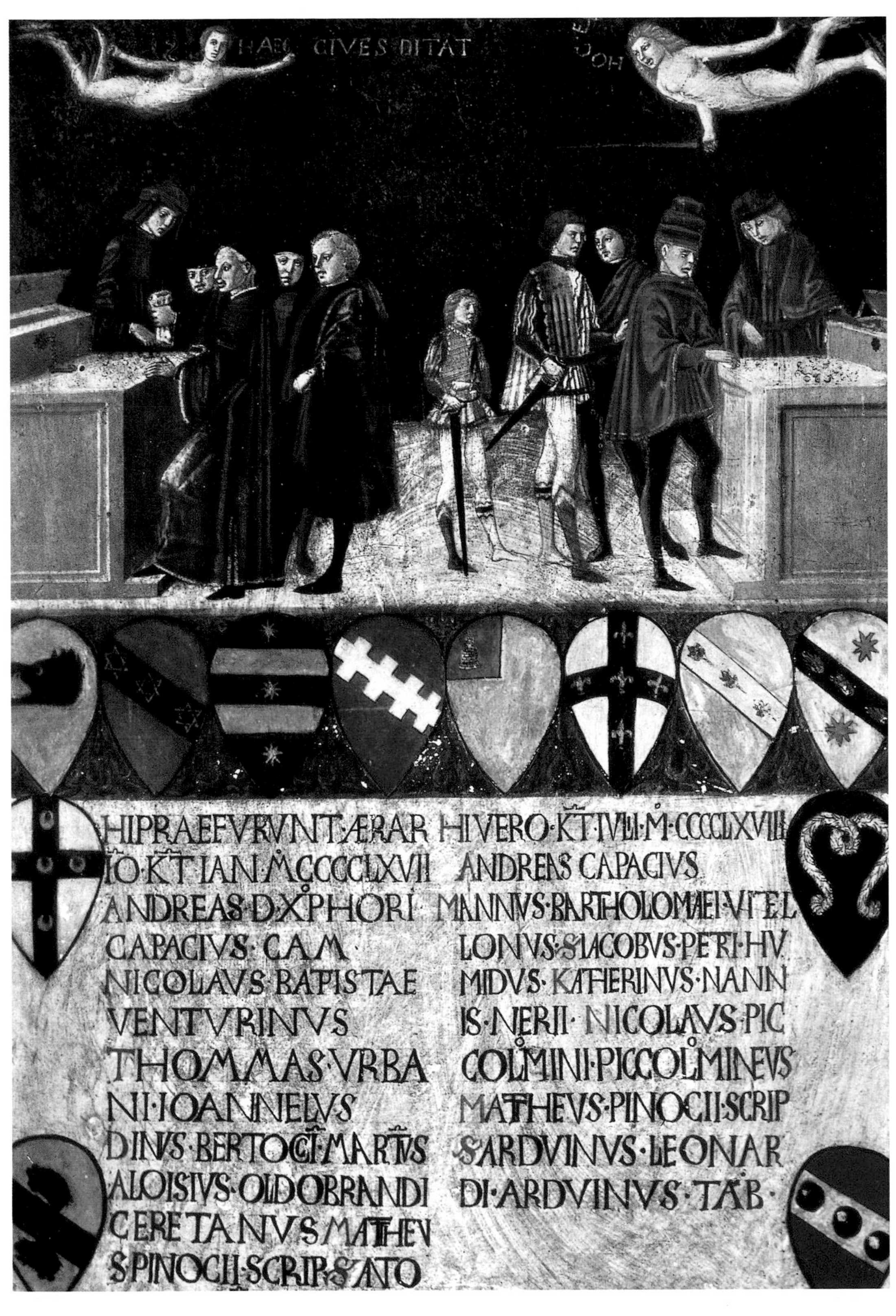

Left: Italian banking firms took charge of the war chests (filled with taxpayers' money). On the right, mercenaries are shown queuing for payment.

Above: Clement IV giving arms to the leaders of the Guelph party, supporters of the papal faction in the struggle with the forces of the Holy Roman Empire.

The Inquisition

The Inquisition was a new organ in Church government, present from the fourth decade of the thirteenth century. Outside Spain, it was not until the sixteenth century that it became a permanent organization with its own body of officials. In the late Middle Ages it was a commission given by the popes to named clerics, to investigate crimes against the faith in particular places.

In the most serious cases the Inquisitors were unable to pass a death sentence, because of the prohibition on clerics from issuing capital sentences, but this, which could not be described with any truth as a moral scruple, was dealt with by handing over the condemned person to lay authorities for punishment. The expected sentence was to be burned alive. However, it should not be supposed that the death sentence was in any way the normal condemnation for all heresy charges; it was not. The question of such punishment differed from the way in which we might expect it to be today, because hardly any medieval penal systems had any provision for imposing a term of imprisonment. Life imprisonment was quite normal, especially for clergy, but a usual lighter penalty in Inquisition courts would have been the obligation to undertake a pilgrimage.

The biggest defect of Inquisition procedures, from the point of view of natural justice, was that they removed from the defendants most of the means of defending themselves that were available either in Roman law or in the various custumary legal systems. The accused were not told

Left: A thirteenth-century fresco from the Palacio Aguilar showing the royal camp of King James of Aragon, who supported the Cathar minority.

intervention, and abandoned too, his long struggle to resist the action of the Inquisition in his territories. As already said, this was a critical period for the Inquisition as an institution since papal commissions of inquisition, which had in the past been issued sporadically, began to be given much more frequently. Generally, in a particular area such as the south of France, the Inquisitors preserved dossiers that could be handed on to later commissioners, so that evidence taken in one trial could be used in later ones. He reluctantly accepted a French royal bridegroom for his daughter and heiress. For the Cathar leadership this was literally a death sentence. In 1243 a royal army attacked the castle of Montségur, where most of the remaining Cathar bishops were, and at the end of a seven-month siege the place fell, on terms that meant the surrender of all the Cathars within it to the Inquisitors. Some Cathar leaders survived, and Catharism continued in Languedoc for a long time, as Emmanuel le Roy Ladourie expounded in his classic book on the mountain village of Montaillou in Foix.[2] But from the death of Raymond of Toulouse in 1249 onwards, the county of Toulouse was a royal fief, which gave full support to the Inquisitors and their formidable archive of denunciations for heresy. Catharism survived among many of the villages of Languedoc, but as a religion of an educated élite it was finished in France, although it survived for a time in Italy.

The relations of the late medieval Church with religious minorities were unhappy, because the assumption that Catholic society was close to divinely revealed truth was so absolute, and was shared at every level of society. The two religious minorities that tested Christendom's stomach for a degree of religious toleration were Jews and Muslims: Jews were present from the beginnings of medieval life; Muslims were present in small numbers after the fall of Islamic Sicily to the Normans in the late eleventh century, and in large numbers after the Christian reconquest of the Iberian peninsula began its final thrust in the early thirteenth century.

Anti-Semitism

The Jews had in the early Middle Ages held a position in Christian society that was on the whole non-segregated, and that allowed them to own and work land, so engaging in the mainstream activities of agriculture. There was plenty of prejudice against them, but it took a very long time to achieve a critical level. The catalyst that set in motion the deterioration of their social position in Europe was the Crusade. The first great massacre of European Jewry occurred at Mainz in 1096, when the archbishop of the city, having tried to protect the Jewish community against the poor 'Crusaders', himself had to flee. Closely similar and equally murderous things accompanied the Second Crusade in 1146, again in the German cities dominated by the higher clergy, although anti-Semitic persecutions were not uncommon elsewhere in Europe. The massacres were at both times connected with radical movements among the poor.

By the early twelfth century, perhaps because of increasing land scarcity, the Jews had been driven out of agriculture, and had become a more or less urban phenomenon – in fact it might be said that the Jewish urban minority was born simultaneously with the European town. In some towns Jews were allowed some self-government, and in others they were allowed to enter civic government alongside Christians; there was for a long time no universal social exclusion. Slight differences between Jewish and Christian religious tradition on how to treat the Old Testament discouragement of usury led to the Jews being more or less driven into the profession of usury, because laws of contract made it increasingly hard for them to continue as merchants.

The rapid economic expansion of Europe meant that society urgently needed a class to facilitate access to credit, and the Jews to some extent supplied that need. Bishops, who were the other great source of ready money, and princes, who saw the possibilities of skimming the profits that Jewish businessmen made from activities that to Christians were illegal, both protected the Jews, though with many reservations. For example, the English King Henry III (1207–72) over a twenty-year period raised more than a third of his cash income from levies ('tallages') on the Jews. This did not mean that the Jews were proto-Rothschilds; the vast majority of Jewish money-lenders were small pawnbrokers.

Christianity was not without its texts to justify anti-Semitic persecution. The basic one was Matthew's apparent attribution of guilt for the crucifixion of Jesus to the Jewish people: 'his blood be on us, and on our children' (Matt. 27: 25) . Latin Christianity had to wait until the end of the twentieth century for its chief bishop to repudiate that interpretation of scripture. There was also John's report (John 8: 37-47) of the debate of Jesus with the Jews in the Temple, in which the demonic element enters

Below: A late fourteenth-century manuscript showing a Jewish pawnbroker at work. Usury and money-lending were illegal for Christians and were often the only way for Jewish people to make a living.

when he says, 'Your father is the Devil... a liar and the father of lies.' Remembering such texts, terrible allegations could ensue, of which the worst was the accusation of ritual murder, first recorded at Norwich in 1144, when the Jews were charged with murdering a Christian child with the object of using the body for satanic rituals.

The Crusades continued to provoke anti-Semitic massacres into the thirteenth century. The attitude of the Church was a little ambiguous. It intervened in their favour against popular fury, and defended them against the charge of ritual murder, but at the Fourth Lateran Council early in the century, which attacked 'Jewish perfidy' in exacting usury, it insisted on their wearing a distinctive dress, and even earlier it had begun in some places to enact the formal requirement that the Jews should at set times listen to Christian sermons aimed at their conversion. There was also prohibition of sexual commerce with Jewish women, and other restriction of social intercourse between Jew and Christian. And in 1239 Pope Gregory IX called in copies of the Jewish religious writings for examination of their doctrines: this was followed three years later by the ceremonial burning of huge numbers of Jewish religious books.

Right: St Louis (Louis IX of France), pious king and lawgiver, was also fiercely anti-Semitic.

Conditions for Jews deteriorated further at the end of the thirteenth century, when the princes who had on the whole protected them began to think that there was more immediate profit and more public approbation to be obtained by expropriating them and expelling them, than by keeping them for further milking. It was possible for them to sacrifice what until that time had been to them a useful and profitable class, because the bankers of central and northern Italy had started to offer the credit and exchange functions that had previously been a Jewish monopoly. This could now be done without formal infringement of the usury prohibition of the Church, because the canon lawyers had found ways to evade it: the pioneers of modern international credit banking were Tuscan banking concerns, which transferred money across Europe on behalf of the popes. England set the trend by expelling all the Jews in 1290, an order that was only formally reversed by Oliver Cromwell, some three and a half centuries later. In France the most pious of its kings, the later-canonized Louis IX (1226–70) was also the most anti-Semitic. His successors drove the Jews from the kingdom in 1306, allowed them to return for a time, and expelled them again in 1322.

The Black Death and its Consequences

The final period of medieval anti-Semitism came with the great agricultural depression and the great plague that took place in the first half of the fourteenth century. The depression was one of under-production and scarcity, beginning with the exceptional bad weather in 1315–17. Many people lived on a subsistence economy off marginal agricultural land, and became indigent as a result. The trend continued; then from 1347 the demographic balance was thrown out by the first of a series of plagues, basically bubonic, that continued at short intervals for a couple of decades, and at rather longer intervals until well into the following century. Population loss was huge, and not restricted to urban areas. In some areas of France and Italy, war devastation added to the problems.

All over Europe, villages in the less productive locations were abandoned. Mortality was greatest among the old and the young – among the young to an extent that cut population replacement. Early population losses of up to a third and more were experienced all over Europe. Labour costs went up sharply, and remained high for about a century. The marginal agricultural land was taken out of production, but the productive farms continued to produce for a smaller market, so cereal prices stayed low, land values fell sharply, and gross national products may have gone down sharply. But, because of population decline, and because also of industrial and commercial resilience, average standards of living probably rose, or at all events rose in some areas. Or putting it slightly differently, people were richer, because they inherited from the plague victims.

The psychological social results of the Black Death (as the disease and population crisis came to be called) have to be sharply distinguished from the economic and the other social results. At birth, life expectation had never been high, but the prospect of sporadic plagues diminished life expectation for the generations that reached maturity. There was at the same time the hope of more money, and the fear of less life in which to enjoy it. *The Decamaron*, a collection of tales by the Florentine writer Boccaccio, recorded the experiences of a group of upper bourgeoisie that had sheltered, hoping to avoid the plague, in a villa in the rich Tuscan countryside. It gives an idea of the comfortable and civilized material environment of the survivors, as well as of their underlying fear.

The religious results of these experiences varied sharply between social groups. At the bottom of society there were dispossession, indigence and despair, all of which encouraged adherence to

extreme religious persuasions. The Flagellant movement was not new: it had originated in the preceding century, and was a movement of mass lay penitence with an apocalyptic message carried in a letter from heaven (such letters had been a frequent vehicle for extreme prophecies of the approaching end of the world, and had figured in eighth-century dissenting movements, and in the crusading propaganda of Peter the Hermit). Its hymn-singing, wandering adherents flogged themselves with spiked scourges in solemn public rituals, convinced that their status absolved them from sin and gave them miraculous powers. Both they and the populations through which they moved thought that their mission was a reproof to a corrupt and ineffective clergy. In 1348–9 there was an especially violent and numerous Flagellant exodus from Germany, with a social-revolutionary impetus that terrified the clergy. When they approached the papal court at Avignon (see below) the pope condemned and dissolved the fraternities, and burned or imprisoned the recalcitrant.

The general direction of religious movements of the late Middle Ages is not easy to gauge. There was a big drift among lay people towards claiming some kind of active participation in church life: through fraternities (of which the Flagellants constituted only a caricature); 'tertiary' or honorary participation in religious orders, especially important among Franciscans; and other organizations represented by all sorts of honorary

Above: Flagellants at Doornik, lacerating themselves to shame a complacent clergy.

Left: A grim contemporary illustration showing the aftermath of the Black Death at Tournai. The plague wiped out whole populations and was blamed on the Jews.

and subscribing adherences, such as those, for example, to the religious crusading orders. The fraternities took part in all sorts of social work, from escorting and comforting condemned criminals to the gallows to ambulance and medical aid organizations, and the ransoming of Muslim prisoners. The great and praiseworthy army of European charity organizations was already in being, although entirely under clerical auspices. There was also a very large number of lay associations of a specifically religious sort, taking part in special devotions and revering especial shrines.

Below: Satan binds the eyes of a Jew. The desire to explain the Black Death led to conspiracy theories, the most persistent of which was the alleged Satanic bargain between Jews and the Devil.

In the closing Middle Ages there was a pious emphasis on human mortality that, in the light of the events of the Black Death, needs no emphasis. The innumerable fresco and sculptural cycles of death and judgement, sometimes in dramatic 'dances', but always emphasizing the fragility of the human body and the imminence of its divine judgement, have exercised a great fascination on modern eyes and minds, although without inspiring a complete understanding of what was involved. For example, these were not dances of death, but dances of the dead. Late medieval Christianity was in some respects a cult of the dead, but one in which the 'art of dying' was to imitate the redemptive death of Jesus. The survivors of the dead could help their lost members by causing memorial masses to be said that would assist their sojourn in purgatory, before their further passage to judgement and redemption.

In the writings of late medieval mystics, especially those of women, there is a parallel awareness, and the same emphasis on the physical details of the body, whether living or decomposing. There can be in all this an element of horror, it is true. To modern minds there can be an extravagance about it that is hard to accept. These passionate saintly women who vomited when sexual contact with their husbands was required, such as Santa Francesca Ponziani of Rome, or who rejected – not from mental instability but from other powerful internal forces – all food, all adornment, all the comforting emotional furniture of family life, may have been revolting against the hard condition of women in their society, but they were also asserting something positive.[4] Their ideals of service and suffering in the imitation of Christ were, moreover, conforming with the main religious currents of their time. It is necessary to emphasize the Christian optimism about the body that informed them. No one, towards the end of the Middle Ages, forgot that the salvation of Christian souls remains the aim of the people of God, nor that salvation, as forecast by St Paul and many others, includes the resurrection of the body.

Demonization

The implications of the Flagellant movement for the Jews were grave. The plague had convinced everyone of divine anger, but at the same time people had an urgent need to find scapegoats. The easiest way to find them was belief in a demonic conspiracy due to an unpopular minority: there had already been in France before the Great Plague a general panic that the lepers had been poisoning the wells, and with this more general crisis it became obvious to huge numbers of people that responsibility for the plague had to be laid at the door of the Jews. If the wells had been poisoned by them all over Europe, then this could only have occurred as a result of a demonic conspiracy. Scripture's ominous references to 'synagogues of Satan' (Rev. 2: 9; 3: 9) were mandate enough to demonize a whole race. As a level-headed student of extremism has written, anti-Semitism has had little to do with conflicts of interest between living people, or even with racial prejudice as such. He sees the popular medieval view of the Jews as being that of '...a league of sorcerers employed by Satan for the spiritual and physical ruination of Christendom'.[3]

All over the Holy Roman Empire, which formed a huge agglomeration of German-speaking and other countries in the centre of Europe, reaching north-west to the Rhine delta, south-west to Provence, there were massacres of Jews. There were frequent efforts by churchmen, in which the pope himself took part, to protect the Jewish communities. It was in itself a human catastrophe, but what was perhaps worse was the failure of the Church to convince Christians in general that the demonization of Jews was wrong. Too many churchmen, especially among the preaching friars, shared the popular prejudices. No authoritative voice was raised high enough to combat the general conviction that Jews were in league with demons.

The Church had had a long history, going back many centuries, of more or less courteous debate with

Above: Universities were advised to teach Hebrew but the virulent anti-Semitic atmosphere of the times made it unpopular.

Left: The statue of the Synagogue in Strasbourg Cathedral, an oasis of calm in a sea of anti-Jewish feeling.

© Palazzo Ducale, Urbino, Italy/Bridgeman Art Library

Right and far right: Paolo Uccello's illustrations show a Christian woman handing over the sacred host to a Jewish pawnbroker as the price for redeeming her cloak. Guards break into the house of the Jew, who, together with his children, is subsequently burned at the stake.

Jewish scholars. In the twelfth century, Peter Abelard had written a remarkable religious discussion that included a Jew: such works were not infrequent, and if they usually showed plenty of prejudice, they were often calm and rational. There was consciousness in the Church of the importance that knowledge of Hebrew could have, both for missionary work and for Biblical scholarship, and at the Council of Vienne in 1311–12 the universities had been advised to set up faculties to teach Hebrew and Arabic – advice that they were careful not to act upon. Right through the Middle Ages, some individual churchmen had friendly relations with learned Jews. But none of this was anything like enough to counteract a poison that worked its way into every part of the body of Christendom.

More than at any previous point in the Middle Ages, the iconic representation of the Jew became coarse and hostile. In the thirteenth-century cathedral of Strasbourg, in what seemed to be traditionally anti-Semitic territory, the statue of the Synagogue could still be tenderly executed, as that of a beautiful, if saddened, woman. But the fourteenth century representations of Jews are particularly distorted and horrible, angry prototypes that were revived in our own times. Perhaps the most frightening of all anti-Semitic pictures, because it is the work of a great Renaissance master, is the fifteenth-century predella by Paolo Ucello depicting a Christian woman who in order to redeem her cloak from a Jewish pawnbroker took him a consecrated host (the sacred element of the Christian Eucharist) to use in satanic practices. When these began, the host bled so that the blood issued under the door of the pawnbroker's house. He was apprehended and the Christian woman was hanged for her part in the affair, although her repentance secured her spiritual salvation. The Jew and his family, including his golden-haired children, are shown being burned at the stake.

© Bibliothèque Nationale, Paris, France/Bridgeman Art Library

Above: Trade between Europe and the Middle East meant that Muslims were slightly more tolerable to Christians than Jews, even though Christians had been, to some extent, persecuted under Islamic rule in Spain.

Christians and Muslims

The corresponding treatment of Muslims by Christians in the lands reconquered from Islam in the Iberian peninsula, while not a model of toleration and kindness, was less drastic than that accorded

to the Jews. There are differing opinions among historians about what happened after the great collapse of Muslim arms in Spain in 1212. It seems most likely that the immediate effects of the Christian occupation of large Muslim areas were catastrophic for the Muslim population, in spite of the facts that some guarantees were given, and that many Muslim potentates made their own bargain with the invaders, sometimes at the price of conversion.

The Christian princes had to tolerate the Muslims to some extent, in order to avoid economic collapse of the lands they cultivated and exploited, and there was a certain give-and-take between the Muslim and the Christian populations. But talk of *convivencia* or coexistence seems exaggerated. As happened to Christians in Islam, public worship by the minority religion was hedged in by restrictions. The call to prayer from minarets was often forbidden in Christendom, just as Christian church bells were often forbidden in Islam. Big mosques became churches, and the funds of Muslim religious foundations were usually confiscated, distinctive clothing was required of Muslims, sexual and marriage alliances forbidden between the religions, all mirror images of what had happened to Christians in Islam.

The most severe aspect of Christian domination concerned the fate of converted Muslims, who were closely supervised, and in the fifteenth century systematically supervised by the Inquisition. Suspected backsliding was punished (as it was also on the part of converted Jews), and frequently followed by execution. For those who continued to be Muslims, the most severe step was expulsion from Christian territory. Some Muslims left voluntarily, following the Qur'anic exhortation to make the flight (*hijra*) incumbent upon Muslims, rather than to accept residence in the lands of unbelievers. But forced mass expulsion, whether or not on the model of that imposed upon Jews in some Christian lands, was another severe sanction. Portuguese rulers resorted to this before the Spanish kingdoms started to think about it in the Renaissance period.

In the fourteenth century the papacy, which had steered a steady course for most of the preceding century, began to feel the pressures exercised by the growing powers of the national state, especially in France and England. It also began, while still powerfully developing its administration and bureaucracy, to lose a certain amount of its moral coherence. Pope Boniface VIII (pope 1294–1303), while a great jurist and administrator, displayed worrying tendencies to behave as a monomaniac dictator (in the modern sense), who placed the interests of his own family above those of the Church. In the latter part of his pontificate, when he was also sick in body, a diplomatic envoy described him as 'nothing but eyes and tongue in a putrefying body... ...a devil'.

The big political problem for the papacy was its inability, after a French prince had occupied southern Italy in 1266, to deal with the French monarchy and its offshoots. Under Boniface VIII the conflict with France became acute, and ended, when the French King Philip the Fair (1268–1314) took an extreme position and demanded the Church condemnation of Boniface and his unseating from the papal throne, in a head-on confrontation between the nascent national state and the papacy. Boniface was overwhelmed by Philip, who sent secret agents to Italy to organize a coup against the pope. In 1303, in the little papal hill town of Anagni, south of Rome, the conspirators seized the person of Pope Boniface in his palace: he died, apparently of shock, a few weeks later.

Babylonian Captivity

In spite of the violent nature of Philip the Fair's victory, it was the prelude to a French domination of the papacy that was unchallenged for three-quarters of a century. In 1309 Pope Clement V (pope 1305–14), who had been born a Gascon subject of the English kings, took up residence in the little city of Avignon, which was technically owned by the popes, and situated just outside French territory, in the 'Kingdom of Arles' that was under imperial and not under French jurisdiction. This was a fig leaf to obscure the political reality of a papacy placed under French protectorate, which endured until 1376. The nature of Philip the Fair's victory became clear after his arrest of the members of the military religious order of Templars throughout his kingdom in 1307, on charges of heresy. In spite of the tendentious nature of Philip's charges, and his dependence upon torture to obtain confessions from some Templars, Pope Clement V was over-persuaded by Philip to act against them at the Church Council held in Vienne (not far from Avignon) in 1311–12, and to dissolve the Templar Order on the grounds of its heresy.

The Roman bishops had for a long time previously been apt to travel far from Rome in the exercise of their duties, and they had occasionally been absent for some years. But the long exile in Avignon was something new in papal history, which could only have occurred as a result of overwhelming domination by a particular Catholic power. Curiously, the only time papal exile outside Italy was ever to be repeated happened when Pope Pius VII was carried off, again to France, by Napoleon in 1804.

Above: Pope Boniface VIII with the College of Cardinals. He was deposed by the French King Philip as a prelude to French control of the papacy.

The 'Babylonian Captivity' (so called from the Biblical parallel of the expulsion of the Jews from Jerusalem and their transfer to Babylon) of the popes at Avignon was especially unwelcome to Italians, although it may be observed that the first peak period of the lucrative predominance of Tuscan bankers at the Roman Court occurred during its residence at Avignon. The efficiency of these bankers in helping papal agents to collect and transmit to Avignon the papal taxes they exacted was a motive for Europe-wide discontent with the papacy on the part of both clergy and laity.

In Rome, the resentment of Romans at the enforced absence of their bishop was manifested particularly during the rule of the so-called Roman tribune, Cola di Rienzo, the flamboyant ruler of the city in 1347, who proclaimed Rome's fame and power in a manner that anticipated the rhetoric of the Renaissance Italian humanists. To symbolize his identification with Christian Rome, he ceremonially bathed in the font of the baptistry of St John Lateran, where, according to legend, Constantine had been baptized. But his rule lasted only a few months.

Italian anger at French 'Babylonian' control of the papacy was expressed by the Florentine proto-humanist poet, Petrarch (1304–74), who complained bitterly of the luxury and corruption of the papal court at Avignon. He denounced its extravagant male fashions – shoes pointed like the prow of a galley, hats with wings, curled hair with long pigtails, men with effeminate ivory combs on their foreheads – and identified the city with the harlot of the apocalypse of St John, who had written on her forehead the mysterious writing, 'Babylon the great, the mother of fornications and the abomination of the earth' (Rev. 17: 1-6).

The Great Schism

Long subjection to French political control, and the long occupation of all the key and best-rewarded offices, from the papacy downwards, by a French clerical élite, weakened the papacy as an institution. The popes at Avignon had recognized that their moral authority in Christendom was compromised by their absence in the Rhone valley, and on one occasion Pope Urban V (1362–70) had made an abortive attempt to return to Italy. At the end of 1376 Urban's successor, Pope Gregory XI (1370–78), landed in Italy, returning finally to Rome in the following year.

After his death in 1378, the first non-French pope to be chosen since 1304, a south-Italian, was elected as Urban VI (pope 1378–89). The big French faction in the College of Cardinals refused to accept defeat, and within a few months elected its own pope, a French-speaking cleric who took the name of Clement VII. Europe almost immediately split into two papal camps, dividing on political lines into pro- and anti-French positions. Within a year or so English troops left for Flanders to fight a Crusade on behalf of their own Pope Urban against his French rival.

Christendom had split along lines that were in part national, and announced the national direction of European politics for the coming centuries. The Latin Church was to remain divided among two, and from 1409 three, papal 'obediences' until 1417. The Church that uniquely prized unity and obedience to a single pastor, in a culture, what is more, that exalted wholeness in all things, was for almost forty years shamefully divided. The blow did not crush the papacy, but the institution was grievously wounded.

1 John Bossy, *Christianity in the West 1400-1700* (Oxford,1985).

2 *Montaillou: Cathars and Catholics in a French Village 1294-1324* (Scolar Press, 1978)

3 Norman Cohn, *Warrant for Genocide: the Myth of the Jewish World Conspiracy and the Protocols of the Elders of Zion* (London, 1967), p.16

4 Caroline Walker Bynum, *Holy Feast and Holy Fast: The Religious Significance of Food to Medieval Woman* (University of California Press, 1987)

4

Imperishable Renaissance Monuments

The papacy was hard hit by the scandals and paradoxes of the Great Schism from 1378–1417. The Schism had been brought to a close by an expedient extremely disagreeable to the popes, that of calling a general council of bishops and other Church dignitaries. The claims of a general council to independent divine inspiration that could even authorize it to take decisions against the will of the person claiming to be God's vicar on earth, were for obvious reasons objectionable. It had been fairly evident from the turn of the fourteenth century that this was going to be the only way out of the schismatic dilemma, but the first attempt at putting it into practice, the council called at Pisa in 1409, failed to impose its solution, and resulted only in raising the number of the contesting popes from two to three.

In 1414 the Emperor Sigismund summoned a general Church council to Constance, which was imperial territory. The more powerful of the two Italian popes, John XXIII (whose reputation for integrity and good conduct was not spotless) was forced by political pressure to attend by his political weakness at the time. In 1415 John was in effect tried for misconduct and deposed. Gregory XII, who had 'been' pope for longer

Left: The Adoration of the Magi *by Gentile da Fabriano (c.1370-1427).*

Above: Mass held by Pope John XXIII at Constance during the Council of Constance held between 1414 and 1418. The illustration, by Ulrich von Riechental, comes from the Council Chronicle.

Right: Before he was deposed at the end of the Great Schism, Pope John XXIII rewarded those who supported him. In this illustration a loyal subject receives a bishopric as cardinals look on.

than John, accepted deposition. The successor of the Avignonese popes, Benedict XIII ('Avignonese' pope from 1394–1424), who had accepted the protection of the King of Aragon, refused to recognize or attend the Council of Constance, but had lost the support of the French bishops, and could only drag out a sulky exile in Spain.

In 1417 the Council of Constance elected a new pope, Martin V (pope 1417–31), a Roman, from among the cardinals of Pope John XXIII. Martin was elected with the support of the English and the Germans, and the consent of the French, and was able to re-establish the Roman papacy. He returned to Rome in 1420. Save for the brief papal exiles of the Napoleonic period, the papacy has remained in Rome ever since. For the rest of the Renaissance period the popes still occasionally wandered elsewhere according to the political and spiritual needs of the times, but far less than in the Middle Ages.

The Council of Constance (1414–18) had been a nightmare for the popes, both those who experienced it and those who came after. One of its closing acts had been to pass a decree requiring the convocation of general council every five years; the popes managed to evade the direct or regular application of this decree, but it remained a threat. 'Reform' had been the watchword at Constance: the council's own efforts in this direction were modest, but it was generally supposed that further councils, in co-operation with the popes, would bring it about. In effect Constance had been the apotheosis of the European universities, which had been directly represented in the sittings, and that had managed (with the co-operation of the English delegation) to impose their own method of corporate governance, that of voting by 'nations', upon the highest authority in the Church. The shadow of nationalism had thus already started to fall over the Church.

The popes who followed the Council of Constance were for a century and a half hag-ridden by the threat of further general Church councils that would allow the secular powers, through their control of their own senior clergy, to decide or strongly influence the destinies of both the popes and the Church. Threats of this sort came from the Council of Basle, which sat from 1431 to 1433 with the consent and to some extent with the co-operation of the pope (Pope Eugenius IV, 1431–47), and for over another ten years without either. In effect the popes were caught in a nationalistic vice: either they accepted Church councils, which claimed almost unlimited powers of Church governance, or they negotiated the affairs of the Church directly with the princely (which with major powers, excepting the Holy Roman Empire, also meant the national) governments through the diplomatic means of 'concordats' or two-party agreements. If the popes wished to govern a national clergy, they were increasingly obliged to do so by making bargains with its princely rulers.

In a Europe that was increasingly dominated by national rivalries, Pope Eugenius IV chose to emphasize the universal and oecumenical perspective of the papacy by negotiating with the Greek Emperor John Palaeologus, who was facing final political and military defeat at the hands of the Ottoman Turks. In turning to the Eastern Church, Eugenius was only following one of the oldest concerns of papal history. In 1274 Pope Gregory X had negotiated with another Palaeologus, Michael, to obtain Greek clerical representation at the Council of Lyons. At that council a form of agreement had been obtained from the Greek delegation that appeared to give their consent to the Western definition of the procession of the Holy Spirit from the Son as well as from the Father (the filioque clause), and so seemed to achieve the reunion of the churches. In Constantinople it proved impossible to persuade the Greek clergy to accept this: the majority of Eastern theologians regarded the filioque clause as a mistaken doctrinal innovation.

Above: Magnificent bronze doors at St Peter's, Rome. Created by Antonio Filarete (c.1400–69), they show scenes from the lives of Christ, the Virgin, St Peter and St Paul, and Pope Eugenius IV.

Something of the same sort happened in 1439. The Greek emperor appeared in Ferrara in north-eastern Italy, where Eugenius had initially summoned the Church council: his arrival is recorded on the great bronze doors cast by the Florentine artist, Filarete (Antonio Averlino, c. 1400–69), for St Peter's, which are still to be seen by anyone who enters the church. The Church council of reunion was prorogued to Florence, the city of Pope Eugenius's Tuscan bankers, the Medici, and the centre of Italian humanism. At this peak moment of the Florentine artistic Renaissance, when Brunelleschi's great dome for the city's cathedral was in the final stage of construction, Eugenius himself had consecrated the church building, three years earlier, in 1436.

In 1439 the council re-assembled there, assured of Florentine financial support. The pope had at his disposal a much stronger negotiating team than any pope of the Middle Ages, since the humanists surrounding the papal curia included some distinguished experts on the Eastern Church. The expectation that humanists were in general a body of people with exclusively this-worldly interests can be disappointed when we look at the Council of Florence, which anticipated some of the arguments about the reunion of Eastern and Western Churches that have resurfaced in our own times. For example, we find at Florence people such as Ambrogio Traversari, the humanist general of the Camaldoli religious order that descended from the eleventh-century hermit, Peter Damian. Traversari was a learned Hellenist, and a scholar of the Greek fathers of the Church, and also a pious ascetic.

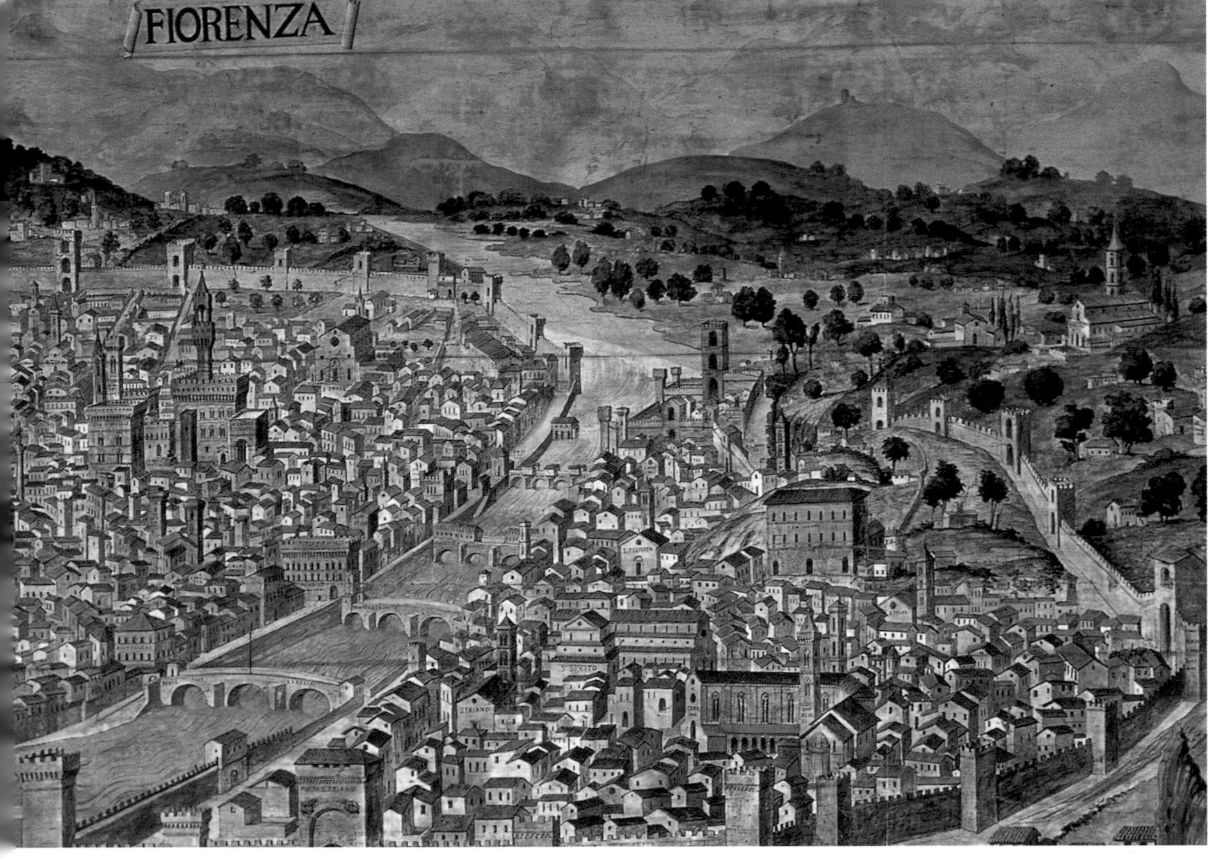

Left: A panoramic view of Florence, the quintessential Renaissance city state, from the Carta della Catena, *1490. Brunelleschi's cathedral dome can be clearly seen in the centre of the picture.*

Below: What had been the Eastern Roman Empire disappeared for ever when Constantinople (Byzantium) fell to the Turks in 1453. This is Tintoretto's version of the event.

Traversari was responsible for drawing up the Greek and Latin texts of the final acts of the Council of Florence.The Greek delegation, which included bishops from the Russian Church, assented to another act of union that, like that of 1274, recognized papal supremacy and consented to the filioque clause. Like its predecessor, this too was rejected by the Greek clergy when the delegation returned to a Constantinople now almost defenceless against the final assaults of Ottoman Turkish power: the end was to come only fourteen years later, in 1453, when Muhammad the Conqueror finally took the city by assault, and put an end for ever to the East Roman Empire.

Renaissance Humanism and the Church

Fifteenth-century Italy was the scene of the greatest effort made in Europe to recover and understand the Greek and Latin heritage. This recovery of classical language and literature had effects far outside the new mastery of the texts. For the first time since late antiquity, educated people began to rediscover a sense of the historical origins of their own culture. To a large extent the architecture and visual arts produced by Italians of that time reflect the understanding of antiquity that had been recovered by the

scholarship that came out of what they called the 'revival of good letters', and that we call 'humanism'.

The new linguistic competence did not, however, mean an immediate revival of the philosophies of the ancient world, in a way that presented an imminent threat to Christian doctrine. Plato, for example, had been an immense influence upon the Christian thought of the Middle Ages, especially during the early and late Middle Ages. The revived Platonic interests of the fifteenth century were intense, and in many ways different, but they could not be said to be unchristian.

The long-term effects of Italian Renaissance humanism were to break the cultural monopoly that the Church had exercised over Christendom since the collapse of the Roman Empire. Breaking the monopoly was a slow process, which required the invention and use of the printing press before it could really take off. Its social achievement was even slower: teachers at Oxford and Cambridge were theoretically still bound by the obligation to clerical celibacy until the second half of the nineteenth century. Over a very long period the new classical humanism was to lead to the displacement of the clerical cultural élite by a lay cultural élite. Democracy, and the erosion of the privileges of the old secular élites by new cadres formed by democratized national education, were to develop only in times relatively close to our own.

By the late Middle Ages lay culture had in many ways been pushed out to the edges of social life. In the fifteenth century it was only genuinely active and powerful in government and the princely courts, in commerce, and in studies such as those of medicine. When it began to return, it was for a long time still in a deferential relationship to the clerks. Only after another couple of centuries was it strong enough to launch what has been called 'the trial of Christianity'.

The idea of the Renaissance is probably now one of the most widely diffused historical notions, but the way people understand it is deeply ambiguous. Greece and Rome have for the past

Right: The great humanist poet Dante, a Guelph sympathizer, reading from his own work, the Divina Commedia. *The poet has been firmly rooted in a Florentine context by the artist, Domenico di Michelino (1417–91). The Brunelleschi dome in Florence, though constructed over a century after the death of Dante, is visible in this picture as it is on that on the preceding page.*

three or four centuries, largely because of the great scholarly efforts of the Renaissance period, been seen as the cradles of the Western human spirit. From the sixteenth century to the mid-twentieth, the texts of ancient Greece were taught in European schools (and when it became relevant, American schools), although only to a limited number of pupils, and the texts of ancient Rome formed part of many secondary curriculums. The Roman Church remains today one of the main citadels where the study of Greek and Latin is defended. But it is rather dishonest to pretend, as is often done, that our modern culture is in some quite direct way based on the classical tradition. The educational method that placed these studies at the centre of the commonly received programme is moribund: both languages are now the concern of a relatively small number of specialists.

The common remark of the medieval universities – 'It's Greek, we can't read it!' – has returned to the modern universities. What has remained of the early modern version of the ancient world for people to admire today is the visual rather than the written legacy. The art of the Italian Renaissance has all the freshness of the new discovery of the ancient monuments and the ancient texts, even for us, most of whom cannot read them. It is still today the object of some of the liveliest interest that modern people can display in their cultural inheritance, as anyone can discover who tries to negotiate the queue to enter the Sistine Chapel in the Vatican in Rome. More people frequent the Italian Renaissance rooms in the big picture galleries than read Machiavelli, and hardly anyone reads Ovid (from whom so many of the Renaissance decorative programmes were taken) or Virgil, or Homer, particularly in their original tongues. A Poet Laureate of the talents of Ted Hughes could manage, at the very end of his life, to make Ovid briefly fashionable through his fine translation of some of the Metamorphoses, but even to highly educated readers much of the Ovidian material is unfamiliar.

The significance of the fifteenth-century scholars who sought out and diffused the many neglected or then unknown ancient texts, lay partly in their independence of the official clerical educational establishment in the universities. That did not mean that they had nothing to do with the Church; on the contrary, many of them were secretaries or other employees of the papal court, and all of them who could, sought out Church benefices of one sort or another, as all learned men of the time did. Nevertheless, in Italy their social context was more the world of the princely courts from which they sought patronage, than the clerical hierarchy.

It is significant that Guarino da Verona (1374–1460), the great educational theorist of the new humanist culture, educated princely and aristocratic children in a school established in his own household. In England in the preceding century the most effective reformer of the old system of secondary education had been Bishop William of Wykeham (c. 1324–1404), who had set up a new kind of residential grammar school or 'college', in order to feed the 'New College' that he had founded in Oxford. Wykeham's foundation was tied into the old university system, although intended also to supply the royal administration with trained clerks. But Wykeham's primary purpose was to supply the Church of God with educated priests: this was not the main aim of the Italian humanist pedagogues.

Christianity was itself the child of late Graeco-Roman culture, and it is probably wrong to start to contrast a 'pagan Renaissance' with a 'Christian Renaissance', as it was usual to do a century ago. On the contrary, one of the main effects of the revival of Greek and Latin studies was to revive the Christian culture of the late Roman Empire, and to bring about a great reassessment of the 'fathers of the Church', and a new understanding of the theology and Church history of the fourth and fifth

Below: A page from the Statutes of New College, founded by William of Wykeham, whose seal as bishop is shown next to the text.

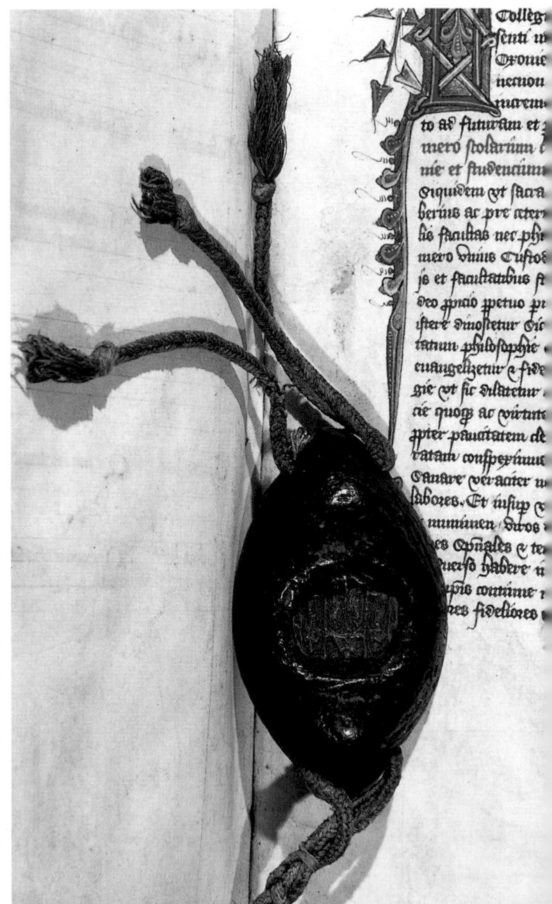

Left: Detail from Michelangelo's fresco the Creation of Adam *in the Sistine Chapel of the Vatican. God and Adam reach towards each other; they are both on the same physical scale, perhaps a metaphor for the growing emphasis that was being put on the human part of the divine plan.*

Right: The architecture of human proportions, Vitruvian Man (c.1492), by Renaissance genius Leonardo da Vinci (1452–1519). Note the mirror writing.

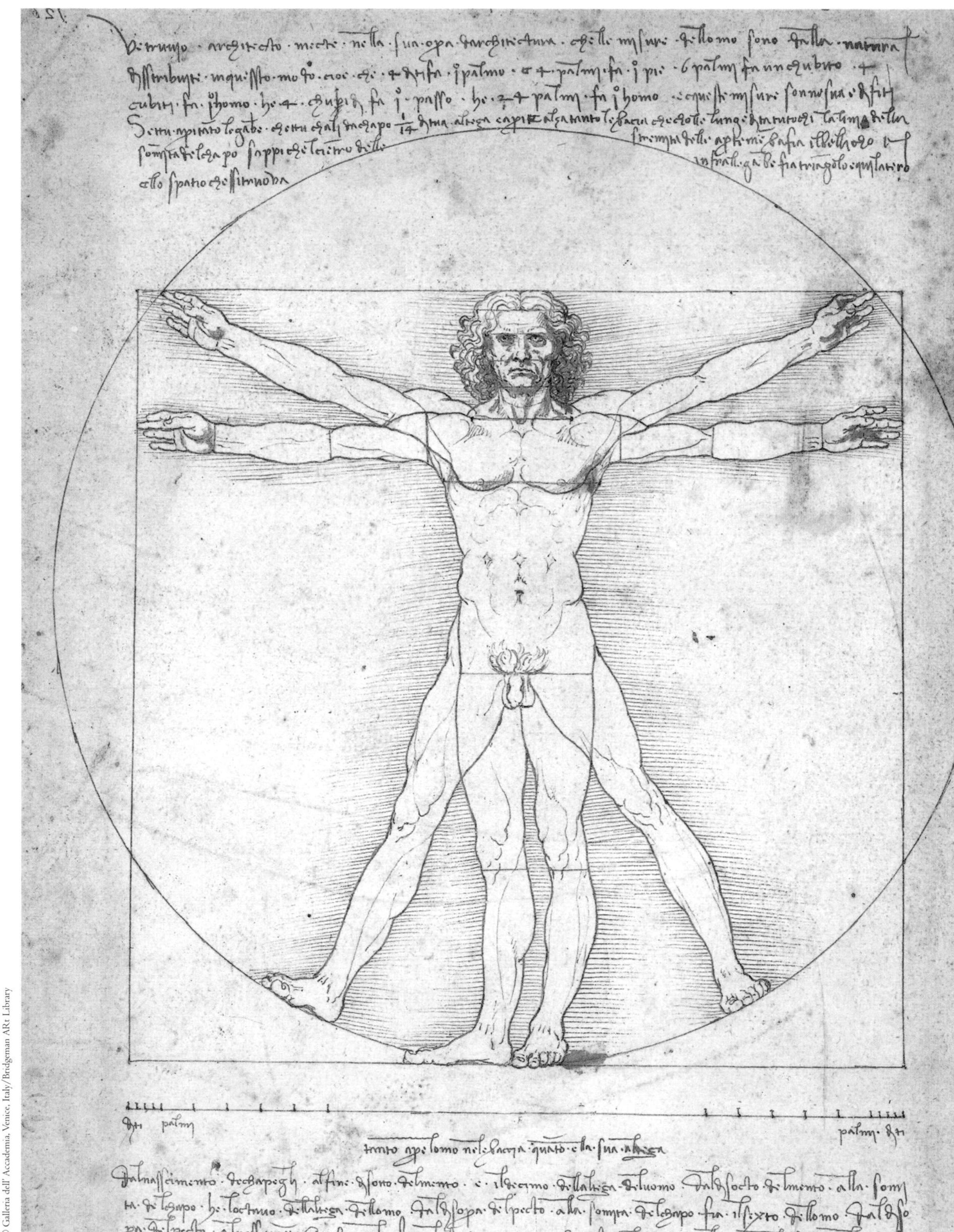

'God the Father, the supreme architect.. therefore took man as a creature of indeterminate nature and, assigning him a place in the middle of the world, addressed him thus: "You, who are confined by no limits, shall determine for yourself your own nature, in accordance with your own free will, in whose hand I have placed you. I have set you at the centre of the world, so that from there you may more easily survey whatever is in the world." ' (Giovanni Pica della Mirandola 'The Dignity of Man')

centuries. It is also a mistake to think that the Renaissance period ushered in anything resembling 'free thought' about religion. It saw a great deal of anticlericalism, and a great deal of irreligious behaviour, but these are not the same as religious disbelief. Looking not at the fifteenth century but at the sixteenth, the great French scholar, Lucien Fébvre, discussed the question in a classic book on the religion of the writer Rabelais. He concluded that there were no real free-thinkers at that period, whether inspired by humanism or by science. As he memorably remarked, it is not so easy for a man to break totally with the habits, the social customs, even the laws of a society of which he forms part, especially when these are all in full force, and when the body of knowledge available to him affords no real solid basis for religious doubt. There were people – of whom Rabelais was one – who could be called free-thinkers for their time, but that does not mean that they were like the free-thinkers of the nineteenth and twentieth centuries. Febvre's view has been challenged since his day, but his main thesis has not, to my knowledge, been disproved.

The Renaissance period inspired and developed a more lively sense of the importance and dignity of man as an individual. The dignity of man had been asserted earlier by the twelfth-century humanists, although, like earlier medieval clerics, they had also emphasized man's moral frailty. Among the Renaissance humanists, and especially among the Platonists, the assertion of human dignity was more definite, and placed in the centre of their theology. The aristocratic Platonist, Giovanni Pico della Mirandola (1463–94), an intellectual prodigy who stood close to the court of Lorenzo de' Medici in Florence, was the author of a speech on 'The Dignity of Man' that had been intended as a preliminary to the nine hundred propositions on philosophy and theology that he offered to defend, as a very young man, and which gained themselves the distinction of being condemned by the pope – although, perhaps because of Giovanni's social distinction, he was not threatened by proceedings for heresy.

The fifteenth-century Church did not, therefore, feel itself threatened by the ideological direction taken by the humanist scholars, who towards the end of the century began to turn their attention to the study of the early 'fathers' of the Church, Latin and Greek, and also towards the renewal of the study of Hebrew. There were some incipient dangers for orthodoxy there, but they took a little time to develop. Dissent and rebellion against the Church very seldom came from such quarters, although they came in from other directions.

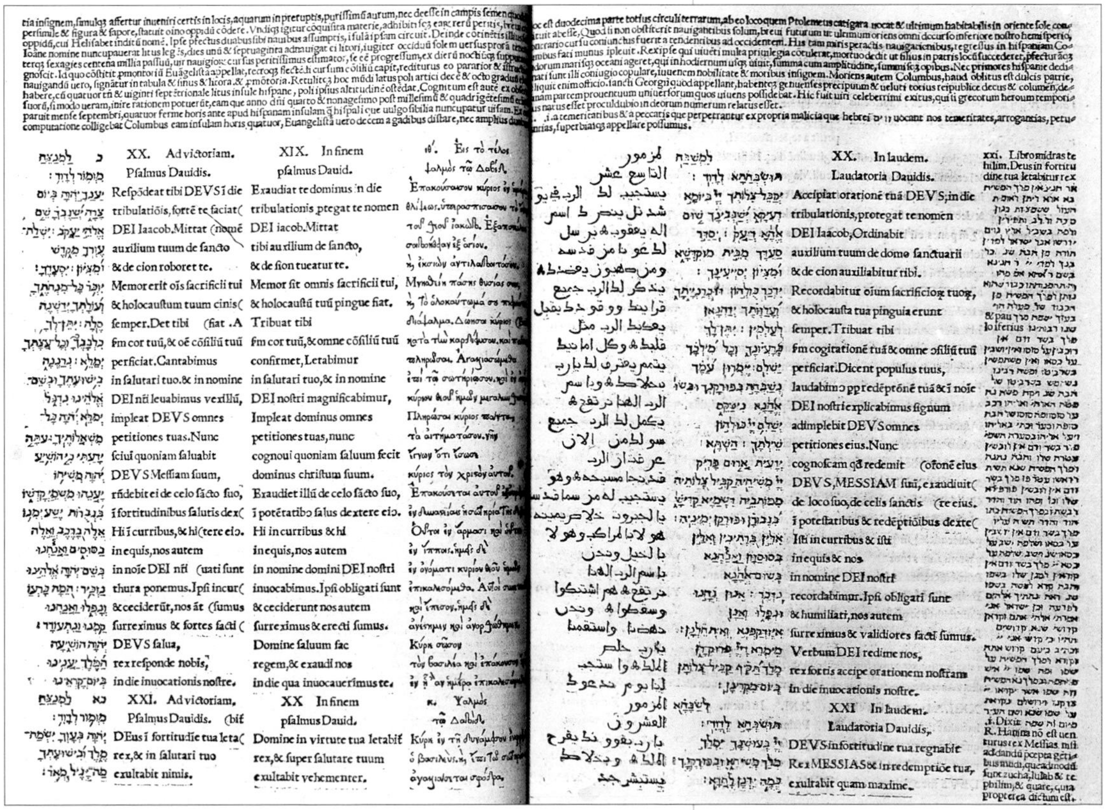

Below: Hebrew version of the Psalms, and parallel translations into Greek, Arabic, Syriac and Latin, edited by Agostino Giustiniani (Genoa, 1516). Humanist scholars reawakened an interest in the languages used by the early Church fathers.

Above: Pius II, regarded as a humanist pope.

Below: The city of Bologna viewed from the observation tower of the university, one of the first to be founded. The astrolabe and ephemeris tables indicate that astronomy was studied here.

The papal court was the major employer of humanists among all the European courts, and by the end of the fifteenth century certain humanist methods and ways of expression had been officially consecrated by the usage of the papal chancery. Humanist Latin and humanist handwriting were obligatory at the papal court by this time for certain classes of papal correspondence. The only spat between popes and humanists was in a way a domestic matter: it concerned the supposedly aggressively pagan 'Academy' set up in Rome by a humanist, Pomponio Leto, in 1468. The 'conspiracy' alleged by the pope of the time to have been the work of humanist academicians seems really to have been concerned with countering papal plans to reduce the salaries of those who were employed as papal civil servants: it concerned labour relations rather than ideology.

Pope Pius II (Aeneas Silvius Piccolomini, pope 1458–64) is widely known as the humanist pope, although the emphatic definite article preceding the appellation is a little odd, since the popes had employed humanists as secretaries and propagandists from the moment that the latter could be said to have existed as a class. Pope Pius II was very far from being the last humanist pope: the successor who perhaps most resembled him in character and interests was Pope Marcellus II, pope for a time in 1555 in the early 'Counter-Reformation'. Papal Rome was the home and protector of humanists until the twentieth century: the humanism of the popes speaks from innumerable churches and public buildings of the city, and can at this day be seen in the fine recent architectural and decorative settings of the Vatican Library.

Scholars, Artists and Patronage

Early humanism depended on princely patronage more than upon anything else. The flourishing state of the Italian princely courts, and the prestige accruing to the patronage of classical learning, enabled the social world of the courtier-humanist to come into being. A few were employed in the Italian universities, which began to set up posts that employed the new style of humanist, but most had to

Left: The Five Masters of Florentine Art: Giotto, Uccello, Donatello, Manetti, Brunelleschi, *an oil painting on wood, c.1450, by one of the subjects, Paolo Uccello (c.1397–1475). Renaissance artists were very dependent on the Church for commissions, or on the patronage of rich families who wished to express their wealth through church decoration.*

look far outside the university world for a career: the university teachers were too wedded to the clerical careers. Only in the case of humanist-lawyers did the two worlds of humanism and university easily overlap. Humanists were valuable to their employer-patrons as propagandists who trumpeted the deeds and importance of their masters to the world in general, and also argued specific political cases for them. They could do this on behalf of the city states, but they acted also as chancellors and general intellectual factotums for the numerous lords and tyrants of the Italian peninsula.

Artists also tended to depend upon princely patronage, but in a more traditional manner than the humanists. At the end of the fifteenth century the new figure of the courtier-artist, who could sometimes even cut a fine figure in the princely court, began to assert itself. Such men were a long way from earlier Florentine artists of at least equal abilities such as Donatello, who had been given a cloak and hood to wear by Cosimo de' Medici, because his patron thought him so shabbily attired, and who then put Cosimo's gift aside because he thought wearing it was too pretentious.

Artists remained, on the whole, tied to the traditional paths of church decoration carried out for the glorification of rich or princely families. The prosperous merchant family in Italy wanted prayer to be made for the protection and salvation of its members in sacred places that were dedicated, if possible, to the privileged use of the family, and to its pride and renown. This was only a continuation of the way in which the rich and powerful had endowed and controlled sacred sites from the beginning of the Middle Ages onwards. Cosimo de' Medici exacted that the Medici coat of arms should be displayed in the Badia of Fiesole and in the church of San Lorenzo that was to be become the great family showpiece. Boasting was the order of the day. Cosimo had the cost of the marble that he paid for Michelozzo to build the tabernacle of the church of the SS Annunziata actually inscribed on the monument. And competition with other rich families was endemic: Benozzo Gozzoli's fresco of the adoration of the Magi in the Medici palace chapel was cribbed from the much earlier Gentile da Fabriano altarpiece in Santa Trinità, commissioned by the great political rivals to the Medici, the Strozzi family.

Below: A seventeenth-century view of St Peter's, Rome, and the Palace containing the Vatican Library, by Gaspar van Wittel (Vanvitelli) (1653–1736).

Right: The coat of arms of the powerful Medici family of Florence, bankers to the popes, patrons of the arts, and political movers and shakers.

Above: The secret account books of Cosimo de' Medici and his grandson Lorenzo 'the Magnificent'. The Medici dynasty was founded by the banker Giovanni (1360–1429), and lasted until the eighteenth century. It was Cosimo who set the pattern for the patronage of art and learning and whose contribution to the Italian Renaissance cannot be underestimated.

The donors often required that their portraits or other representations should be included in the chapel or church concerned, associated with the depiction of the patron saint or other religious object that was involved. Such arrangements of donor and dedicatee could be found in Renaissance Italy, and in churches all over Europe. And the donor was not necessarily a family or a family head: the very numerous religious confraternities also endowed chantries and chapels in the same ways and with the same objects. Most of the adult male population in the towns might have been expected to belong to one religious confraternity or another.

Imperishable Monuments

Humanism was not an ideology, but a body of literary and philological knowledge, which could be put to propagandist use to support whatever ideas were chosen. The oldest and most powerful ideology was still that of the Church, and humanism was naturally placed at the service of the Renaissance Church. This was far from being a strange adventure for the clerical apologists, since there had been a continuous tradition of learned praise for the Church, which stretched back into late antiquity.

The first pope to use the whole humanist propagandist machine in a conscious way in the service of the Church, and to gear it also to a big architectural and urbanist programme, was Pope Nicholas V in the mid-fifteenth century. The papal court was well served by humanists throughout the period; over the fifteenth century about eighteen per cent of papal secretaries were well-known

Left: The interior of the Chapel of the Princes, San Lorenzo, Florence showing the altar flanked by the tombs of two later Medicis, Cosimo I, 'the Great' (1519–74) and Ferdinand (1549–1609).

Below: Detail from the altarpiece in Santa Trinità. The Adoration of the Magi *(1423) by Gentile da Fabriano (c.1370–1427), at the commission of the Strozzi family, rivals to the Medicis.*

Below: A papal benediction in the square of St Peter's Church in Rome. In the background, the new dome is being built. Luther was outraged by the huge amounts that the popes spent on architectural splendour.

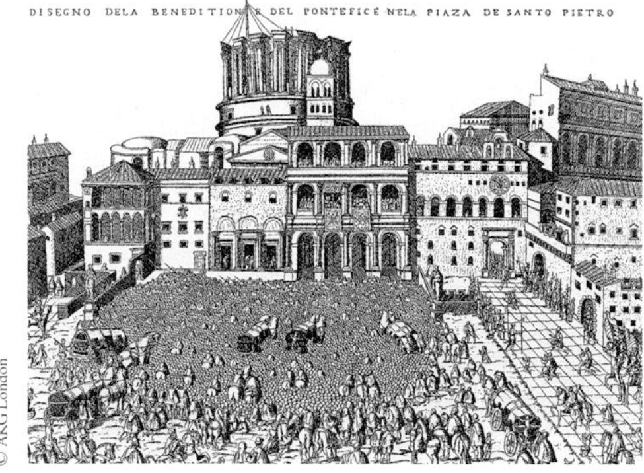

Below: Pope Sixtus IV installing Bartolommeo Platina as Librarian of the Vatican Library. The fresco is by Melozzo da Forli (1438–94).

Greek or Latin scholars, and one secretary in four corresponded on his own account with other learned humanists. Pope Nicholas V began the long process of the re-planning of St Peter's, which lasted, with many long interruptions, until the beginning of the seventeenth century, and whose execution was to cost huge sums of money. The expenditure figured among the grievances that caused Luther's rebellion against Church authority in the early sixteenth century.

Pope Nicholas V employed the Florentine humanist Gianozzo Manetti (1396–1459), the author of a tract on the dignity and excellence of man, inferior in scope and talent to the later tract of Giovanni Pico della Mirandola, and written in a rather more conformist spirit. Manetti was Nicholas's biographer, and he recorded his papal patron's view, which he not very convincingly says was pronounced on the pope's death-bed, that:

> *'Only the learned who have studied the origin and development of the authority of the Roman Church can really understand its greatness. Thus, to create solid and stable convictions in the minds of the uncultured masses, there must be something which appeals to the eye; a popular faith, sustained only on doctrines, will never be anything but feeble and vacillating. But if the authority of the Holy See were visibly displayed in majestic buildings, imperishable memorials and witnesses seemingly planted by the hand of God himself, belief would grow and strengthen from one generation to another, and all the world would accept and revere it. Noble edifices combining taste and beauty with imposing proportions would immensely conduce to the exaltation of the chair of St Peter.'*

'Taste and beauty' meant that aesthetic standards would be imposed upon the papal propagandist programmes by the educated and cultured, in other words, that humanist taste would dictate them. The papal court was for the rest of the century equal to and probably superior to any other European court as a centre of humanist culture and excellence. The relationship between papacy and culture is unforgettably illustrated by the 1475 fresco by Melozzo da Forlì (now in the Vatican Gallery), which shows Pope Sixtus IV (1471–84) among his court scholars and his nephews, naming Bartolomeo Platina, the historian of the popes, Librarian of the Vatican Library.

The papal programmes of urban renewal for the city of Rome, which started the fifteenth century as a great farmyard full of classical ruins, and which even at its end was still a city of medieval towers, in general appearance not unlike – in part, at least – the present Tuscan town of San Gimignano, began to develop seriously under Pope Julius II (pope from 1503–13). He was the nephew of Pope Sixtus IV, as an inscription two or three metres tall still tells us from the outer wall of the great papal Belvedere. It was Pope Julius II who commissioned the Lombard architect, Bramante, to prepare the first plans for the great new church of St Peter, recorded in a papal medal of the time. The

Left: Interior of St Peter's, Rome. The building of this great basilica engaged the talents of almost every major Renaissance architect, including Bramante, both Sangallos, Raphael, Peruzzi, Michelangelo, della Porta, Fontana, Vignola and Bernini. The dome shown here was designed by Michelangelo and executed by della Porta, and the canopy is the creation of Bernini.

Above: A late fifteenth-century engraving of Rome at the end of the Middle Ages.

Below: The School of Athens, *a fresco made between 1510–11 by Raphael (1483–1520). Plato (modelled by the artist on Leonardo) and Aristotle can be seen in the centre of the picture. The Renaissance in Rome was led by the humanist Pope Nicolas V, many of whose staff were Latin or Greek scholars.*

construction of Bramante's proposed new church entailed the entire demolition of the old basilica of Constantine. It is not much remarked in modern times that the Rome of Raphael and Michelangelo saw one of the most ruthless campaigns for the destruction of ancient monuments in recorded history. Much of ancient Rome was literally ground to powder and burned, to provide the mortar to build Renaissance Rome.

The Unarmed Prophet: Savonarola

Girolamo Savonarola (1452–98) was a Lombard Dominican preacher brought up in Ferrara. His prominence in Florentine history, and in Church history in general, is owed to the accident that he happened to be have been a very fashionable preacher, and the prior of the Dominican convent of San Marco in Florence, favoured by the dominant Medici dynasty, at the moment of the French military intervention in Italy in 1494 that transformed Italian political life.

The invasion of Italy by the French King Charles VIII in 1494, in pursuit of a claim to the throne of the kingdom of Naples (which was to be extended by his successor to include a claim to the duchy of Milan), was a revival of French dynastic ambitions in Italy that went back to the thirteenth century. It was countered in due course by a revival of Spanish (or more narrowly, Aragonese) traditional dynastic claims in Italy, which led to long and destructive wars in the Italian peninsula between the two powers. In one way or another the wars dragged on until the middle of the sixteenth century. By the time they were over, the decentralized communal and regional independence that had marked much of Italian political life in the late medieval and earlier Renaissance period was finished, and Italy had to submit to the dominance of an external great power (Spain) and to the predominance of a much more centralized and formalized princely domination over its regional governments.

The domination of the Medici family over Florence and its subordinate zone of Tuscany had until the French wars been a delicately balanced affair, which had preserved the fiction of communal constitutional government, and represented the Medici rulers as being little more than the influential first citizens of the republic. In 1494 the approach of the French armies of Charles VIII, who had been opposed by the Florentine government in power, led to the immediate destabilization of the latter. The able and gifted Lorenzo de' Medici had died young in 1492. His son Piero, who lacked all his father's political abilities, was in short order expelled from the city, and, after a very brief French occupation, what was left of the Medici regime collapsed.

Savonarola emerged immediately as the most prominent figure of the post-Medici regime that occupied the political vacuum which occurred after the French withdrawal. It was a weak regime that depended fundamentally upon a coalition of the Florentine oligarchs most opposed to the Medicis. It spoke the language of a restoration of Florentine republicanism, and made constitutional changes intended to effect this, which to a very limited extent copied Venetian models.

Like many spokesmen for the ideologies of restored conservatism, Savonarola (who occupied no permanent political post) argued very loudly for religious revival and moral rearmament. He was fully in the tradition of the revivalist preaching of the friars of his period, who were accustomed, almost always with the approval of their governments, to call for a new attitude of high moral seriousness to the responsibilities of communal politics. Using the pulpit as a fulcrum of the regime was no novelty. An argumentative but eloquent man, he was able to win followers over a very wide range of opinions and groupings, including some distinguished humanists: his supporters were known as Piagnoni (Pious Whiners).

The government, under Savonarola's influence, had severe laws enacted against blasphemy, sodomy – supposed to have been a widespread Florentine practice – and ostentatious frippery; the friar inspired the setting up of a morals police force at street level. His tactics included the organizing of great 'bonfires of the vanities' in which penitents (assisted by the blackmailing of the morals police) publicly burned the symbols of their proud and sinful conduct. These street dramas served to dramatize Savonarola's message and to entertain the public.

Savonarola was a formidable man. A person who could get himself treated posthumously as a major political factor by Machiavelli and attract the loyalties of Michelangelo, besides inspiring the Christian Democrat mayor of Florence in the 1950s, Giorgio la Pira, to sleep in his cell in search of holiness and inspiration, cannot have been a nonentity. He saw himself as a prophet, perhaps even as a Moses who would lead the Florentines out of the wilderness to the holy land. His prophecies were in part political: they saw the French king as a sort of Nebuchadnezzar whose power would lead to a millennial judgement (perhaps to take place in 1500) on the peoples of Italy, and to a great restoration of the spiritual Church. At a time when millennial anticipation of the end of all things was widespread, when engravings were made of a monster with the head of an ass and the body of a woman, said to have been found on the banks of the flooded River Tiber in Rome, beside the papal castle of Sant'Angelo, the pronouncements of Savonarola were readily heard.

He was no proto-Protestant: to the day of his death Savonarola saw himself as an orthodox member of a strict religious order. But in common with large numbers of people of his time, he saw the papal regime in Rome as corrupt. Pope Alexander VI (Alexander Borgia, pope 1492–1503) was the nephew of a rigorist Spanish pope, and for a long time before acceding to the papal office had been head of the papal civil service, the papal vice-chancellor. His sexual morals were certainly lax before, and very probably after, becoming pope, and he caused scandal by the political powers and the special place in his court that he accorded to his daughter, Lucrezia. His nepotism, and the ruthless and often murderous conduct of his son, Cesare, had so many precedents among earlier papal uncles and nephews that it is hard to see them as particularly shocking, and indeed the ruthlessness of Cesare is allowed to have been of probable long-term benefit to the papal state.

The puritanical eloquence of Savonarola would have no truck with the vain ecclesiastical pomp of Rome and elsewhere – for Venice and London were then held to be just as remarkable for solemn and seemly church ceremony as Rome.

After a couple of years Savonarola became unacceptable to Pope Alexander VI, not so much because of his moralistic sermons but because of his pro-French foreign policy. He also became a great deal less acceptable to the Florentines, because of the failure of the pietist government to obtain the submission of the Florentine subject-city of Pisa, which had rebelled after the first French withdrawal in 1494. The pope had plenty of weapons to use against a truculent friar; after some manoeuvring he used the most powerful, his condemnation for doctrinal unorthodoxy. The weakening political position of the Florentine republican government meant that it would no longer protect Savonarola from

Below: This portrait of a woman by Bartolommeo da Venezia (fl. 1502–46 in Ferrara) is thought to be the likeness of the notorious Lucrezia Borgia, sister to Cesare and daughter of the corrupt pope Alexander VI (Rodrigo de Borgia). Married to a series of ever more politically powerful husbands, she ended her life as the Duchess of Ferrara.

Church disciplinary measures. Excommunicated, he appealed to the judgement of a future Church council; it was a legal device invoked by many Church reformers, subsequently including Luther. In 1498, papal commissioners arrived in Florence to proceed to his trial, which ended in his being declared heretical and schismatic. He and his two closest supporters among the friars were hanged, and their bodies burned, all in the public square of the Signoria. As has often been remarked, the burning of the friars replaced the burning of the vanities.

The echoes of the Savonarola controversy continued to sound among the religious disputes of the sixteenth century. But neither they, nor the many other voices of protest and doubt in Italy, were ever to lead to a viable Italian Protestantism. The only firm line of anti-papal protest in Italy, the 'Waldensian' protest of the north Italian hills, had medieval roots, and was firmly established before Savonarola was even born. Savonarola was too deeply rooted in the political issues of provincial Italy to go very far in generalizing the theological issues of his own evangelism. He remained to his death a city preacher, who needed the approval of the surrounding urban society in order to transmit his message. In parts of Germany, a generation later, the city fathers proved willing to turn publicly to Luther: in Italy this did not happen. There was dissent against the Church in Renaissance Italy, but neither Savonarola, nor the religious rebels of the following century, managed to transform it into a revolutionary force.

Right: An unknown Italian artist has chronicled the torture and death of Savonarola, the charismatic preacher and religious reformer who was hanged and burned for heresy and sedition.

'Men feed upon these vanities and rejoice in these pomps, and say that the Church of Christ was never so flourishing, nor divine worship so well conducted as at present... ...In the primitive church the chalices were of wood, the prelates of gold; in these days the church has chalices of gold and prelates of wood. These have introduced devilish games among us; they have no belief in God, and jeer at the mysteries of our faith.. ..Arise, and come to deliver thy Church from the hands of devils, from the hands of tyrants, the hands of iniquitous prelates.'
(Savonarola's Advent Sermon)

Left: Portrait of Girolamo Savonarola (1452–98), the 'puritan of Catholicism' whose philosophy opposed the humanist revival fuelled by the Medicis.

5

REFORM

In 1512 the warrior-pope Julius II, still at war with the French armies in Italy, had called the Fifth Lateran Council in Rome.The opening speech of the Council was pronounced by the talented head of the monastic Augustinian Order, of which friar Martin Luther was already a member. In his speech the Augustinian general, Giles of Viterbo, said that men must be changed by religion, not religion by men.

Within twenty-five years of the delivery of that speech, new 'Protestant' churches that utterly rejected the papacy and most of its key doctrines had been set up with the approval and support of the princes, in Germany and other parts of the Empire, in Scandinavia, in England. In 1536 the French reformer, Jean (John) Calvin (1509–64), then established in Basle, addressed the French King Francis I in the dedicatory preface to his *Institutes of the Christian Religion*. He asked the king to recognize that the doctrine whereby popes, cardinals, bishops, abbots and priests claimed to be the Church, was itself a deadly butchery of souls, a firebrand, a ruin, and a destruction of the Church. How had this revolutionary state of affairs come about?

The idea of an urgent, approaching general reform of the Church 'in its head and its members' had been firmly rooted in late medieval Christianity since the beginning of the fifteenth century, when Church councils had managed to end the Great

Above: A seventeenth-century portrait of the French theologian Jean (John) Calvin.

Left: The Council of Trent, 1563.

Above: Raphael's portrait of Pope Julius II, instigator of the Fifth Lateran Council, at which Martin Luther spoke.

Above: Pope Leo X, the Medici pope who succeeded Julius II, bracketed by Cardinal Luigi de'Rossi and Giulio de Medici. The portrait is by the Renaissance master, Sanzio Raphael (1483–1520).

Schism of the papacy, but not to go much further. It was the councils, above all, which had created the expectation of such reform, but by the end of that century the Church leadership had signally failed to deliver it. It was an ideal to which the Borgia Pope Alexander VI had paid lip service – and even, in the months that followed the murder of his son, the Duke of Gandia, a little more than lip service. To some extent the reform idea was present in the Fifth Lateran Council, although the reform provisions of that council were pale and ineffective, like so many earlier half-measures. In 1517 the Council was closed by the Medici Pope Leo X (pope 1513–21), who succeeded Julius.

To create a general expectation within a polity, and then continually to postpone and procrastinate about it, is recognized in our own times as a way of allowing revolutionary demands to reach the point of explosion. In sixteenth-century Europe no one had formulated such an analysis, which went against the prevailing cosmological model of a hierarchy of divinely sanctioned powers. It was a theory still eloquently argued by William Shakespeare at the beginning of the following century, in the great speech about order and degree that he assigned to Ulysses in *Troilus and Cressida*:

...Degree being vizarded,
Th'unworthiest shows as fairly in the mask.
The heavens themselves, the planets and this centre,
Observe degree, priority and place,
Insisture, course, proportion, season, form,
Office and custom, all in line of order;...
... O, when degree is shak'd,
Which is the ladder of all high designs,
The enterprise is sick! How could communities,
Degrees in schools, and brotherhoods in cities,
Peaceful commerce from dividable shores,
The primogenity and due of birth,
Prerogative of age, crowns, sceptres, laurels,
But by degree, stand in authentic place ?
Take but degree away, untune that string,
And hark, what discord follows !

[Act I Sc iii]

Religious Rebellion

The repudiation, on the part of many Christian peoples, of the fundamental hierarchy of government in Christendom, in a society that professed such principles, could only have come about at the end of a long period of preparation and drift. The fifteenth century had been, it is true, rather less troubled by really radical religious movements than the thirteenth and fourteenth, but there had been a gradually increasing demand for active lay participation in religious life. Movements such as that in the Low Countries of the so-called 'modern devotion' may have proved more effective in shifting fundamental religious attitudes than the 'heretical' efforts of people who tried to mount head-on assaults on Church authority. 'Modern devotion' called for religious inspiration in all the ordinary affairs of a lay person's life, a call that applied to women equally with men. A classic manual of the movement that is still alive in Christian practice is the *Imitation of Christ*.

There were also certain ideological clefts in the religion, which enabled cataclysmic sacred events to be envisaged. Of these one of the most important was certainly the eschatological expectation of the end of all things that was written indelibly into the Book of Revelation, and present in other parts of the New and Old Testaments. Behind this lay three centuries of such

Left: The Preaching of the Antichrist, considered a sign of the imminent apocalypse, depicted in a fresco by Luca Signorelli (c.1450–1523) in the San Brixio chapel at Orvieto Cathedral.

Above: An image from John Foxe's Acts and Monuments, *1563. It shows the 'Hanging and Burning of Diverse Persons counted for Lollards, in the First Year of the reign of King Henry V'.*

expectations, which bore the mark also of the late twelfth-century Cistercian abbot and mystic Joachim of Flora (c.1135–1202), who had predicted the onset of a new era of the Spirit, to begin in 1260. The turn of the fifteenth century, as always, was a period when millennial expectation was very widely diffused. No one can look at the great fresco by the Italian artist, Luca Signorelli (c.1441–1523), in the cathedral of Orvieto, that represents the manifestation of Antichrist at the end of time, without experiencing something of the disturbance and terror of the apocalyptic vision.

There was also, by the end of the fifteenth century, the knowledge that there had already been a successful national religious rebellion. 'Hussitism' in Bohemia had actually established itself as a slightly divergent confession, which had managed to squeeze partial recognition from the official papal leadership. The great Czech religious reformer Jan (John) Hus (c.1372–1415) had been burned as a heretic by the Council of Constance in 1415, and the English 'Lollard' followers of his similar and older English contemporary, John Wyclif (c.1330–84) had been similarly persecuted and kept down. Both the English and the Czech movements owed quite a lot to theological doctrines taught in the universities. But they also had a popular base. In England this was the vernacular translation of the Bible; in Bohemia sentiment tended to find a central point in the demand for giving the cup of consecrated wine to the laity, as well as the consecrated host, when Communion was administered. The Czechs had resisted a bloodthirsty papalist 'Crusade' against them in the 1420s, in which English troops had taken part. In the end a very moderate Hussite or 'Utraquist' Church (that administered the sacraments in both kinds) had survived in Bohemia. It had wrung a very reluctant consent from the popes to lay participation in the cup, and this was its only major divergence from Catholic practice. The 'Bohemian Brethren', who professed a more radical reformist doctrine than the Hussites, had also survived.

It could have been argued on behalf of the Roman Court that a very large part of the centralized regime of papal taxation and Church appointments that aroused so much resentment in the later Middle Ages had been set up in direct response to the demands of local clerical oligarchies. Fundamentally a Church benefice, a category of Church office that included the care of parishes, but could be applied also to many other duties and dignities, was the object of private rights and not of public interests. This remained true in Protestant England, for example, until the nineteenth century. These demands had come particularly from the universities, which made such loud protests against the system in Church councils, and from the princes, who liked to give the impression that they shared nationalist resentments against Rome, while in fact they profited from Roman compliance with their wishes. The popes managed a market, but they could not have done so if the demand for the goods – in this case, Church benefices – had not existed. The endless manuscript rolls of petitions to the popes that are still recorded in the Vatican archives prove that this was so.

The critical issue, as in so many similar situations where an ancient organization defends itself against outside pressures, was the boundary between reform and rejection of the system. Like many very large and conservative bodies, the papacy was unable to deal with its own gravest problems. The real question, it already seemed to a German reformer in the Roman Court before 1400, was not whether the popes were abusing their powers, but whether they had usurped powers to which they had no right.[1] Significantly, Dietrich of Niem never pressed his question to its logical conclusion. He was an upright man, but also an important lawyer-administrator within the papal system and a connoisseur of southern Italian wines.

Sin and Salvation

Men and women need to be able to engage in some kind of transaction to try to settle the disquiet they so often experience about the way in which they manage their lives. The manner in which they experience this disquiet changes from one historical time to another, and so does the form of the transaction. In the century now ending, people in the Western world have sometimes turned to the methods proposed by Sigmund Freud: in late medieval Christendom they used the machinery of penance, very different from that in use earlier in the Middle Ages, which had been set up after the momentous requirement of annual sacramental private penance and of public sacramental reconciliation that had been established by the Fourth Lateran Council in 1215.

In the sacrament of penance there were elements of personal conversion and of submission to the divine will. But these elements were too often submerged in the formality of the occasions, which in many cases responded to the requirements of Church law rather than to the needs of individual conscience. People were conscious of these discrepancies, though not often in an analytic way. That serious discontent with the penitential regime of the Church was frequent is certain; that it was universal throughout Christendom is a great deal less certain.

In any examination of the factors that led to the 'Protestant' reform of considerable areas of Christendom in the sixteenth century, it has to be emphasized at the start that loyalty to the Catholic Church turned out, in the course of that century, to be more frequent than disloyalty. Many things of a completely secular nature were of immense weight in deciding the issue, most of all the allegiances of the princes. But the survival of majority Catholicism in Europe, which also decided much of what was to happen in the New Worlds, has to be recognized.

Indulgences, or clerically authorized remission of some of the penances required for sin, were tightly connected with the regime of penance. The most innovative transaction among them, which St Bernard himself had compared to a commercial transaction, had been the introduction of indulgence

Below: Detail from a triptych of 1547 in the church of St Marien, Wittenberg, by Lucas Cranach the Elder. It shows Martin Luther preaching.

© Galleria degli Uffizi, Florence, Italy/Bridgeman Art Library

Above: Portrait of Martin Luther by Lucas Cranach the Elder (1472–1553).

Below: Erasmus of Rotterdam, Europe's greatest humanist, after Hans Holbein the Younger.

© Hermitage, St Petersburg, Russia/Bridgeman Art Library

for sins as a reward for the pilgrimage of the Crusade, which had first appeared at the Council of Clermont in 1095. Late medieval indulgences were multiform, but they were often issued in exchange for contributions to church building funds, as was the case with the indulgences issued by Pope Leo X in 1517 to finance the rebuilding of St Peter's in Rome. To the preaching of this indulgence in Germany, the German Augustinian friar and theology professor, Martin Luther (1483–1546), published a shocked objection in the Saxon town of Wittenberg, in the same year. The objection formed part of a number of protests against clerical abuses, and a statement of his theological grounds, all cast in the academic form of 'theses', but still marked by the idiomatic power of expression that characterized all Luther's polemics.

In so far as Luther was a revolutionary, he was a remarkably unsystematic one, and the more so early in his career. What he denounced in 1517 was not the power of the visible Church to represent Christ, but the abuse by which the pope purported to remit the penalties of sin without calling for contrition on the part of the sinner. From this premise, which to modern eyes may seem still to be a conservative one, Luther moved by stages to a rather more radical position. At the heart of his theology lay the words of St Paul (Romans I: 16–17) that the Gospel is the saving power of God for everyone who has faith: God's righteousness starts from faith and ends in faith. In this conviction lay the eventual condemnation, in Luther's eyes, of the entire priest-mediated penitential and sacramental system. In choosing Paul as the greatest of Christ's apostles, Luther was following mainstream humanist opinion of his age.

In 1520, after the failure of quite a lot of diplomatic wheeling and dealing on the part of a Roman Court that was rightly rather fearful of German public opinion, Luther was excommunicated. By this time he had secured the support of his own Saxon Electoral Duke, and of important sections of the West German nobles: as his case became a well-publicized issue, so also he secured a larger and larger following in the German cities.

The Word of God and the Printed Word

'The climate of opinion' is a treacherous and slippery phrase, but there is no doubt that that in the crucial few years between 1517 and 1525 Luther identified the *Zeitgeist* in Germany, and critically influenced it. He did so partly from a political position that turned out to be very influential among the German princes, and partly by using the new technology of the printing press. The pamphlets he wrote at this time, such as *The Babylonian Captivity of the Church, On the Freedom of a Christian Man,* and *To the Christian Nobility of the German Nation,* are among the most influential publications of modern Christian history. In the first of these the break with Rome was already defined as final. The pope was 'a man of sin and a son of perdition who sits in the Church like God, and by his doctrines and statutes increases the sin of the world and the destruction of souls'.

Appearing in 1521 in Augsburg before the German Emperor Charles V(emperor 1519–55) and the Imperial Diet to answer the charges against him, Luther refused to withdraw from his position, and dramatized his case before the German nation. He also calculated correctly that his political support was strong enough to discourage Charles V from repeating the acts of the Emperor Sigismund who, in 1415, had ignored the safe-conduct that he had granted and allowed the Council of Constance to burn the reformer John Hus.

Luther and like-minded reformers depended upon the word of God. But the word of God could only be known through the right understanding of the texts of the Scriptures, and such

understanding demanded knowledge that could only be supplied the by humanist philology of Hellenists and Hebrew scholars. The greatest of all northern European humanists, Erasmus of Rotterdam (c.1466–1536), far the greatest man to come out of the 'new' or 'modern devotion' in the Netherlands, gave the reforming milieu his translations of the Greek fathers of the Church and of the New Testament. His commonplaces also supplied a new Christian humanist point of view. 'Dogma did not engender faith; faith came before dogma' was an observation of Erasmus.

Above: The Day of Pentecost, when believers spoke in tongues (shown by the flames coming from their mouths) from Luther's translation of the Bible into German (c. 1530). The papal dragon is powerless to interfere.

Sixteenth-century biblical criticism did not begin as a movement to bring the word of God straight to the people, although it was a necessary preliminary to such a movement. It was, on the contrary, a part of a cult of passionate humanist élitism. Modern disparaging ideas about 'popular religion' derive in part from the scorn shown by Erasmus, who wrote:

> *'One who aspires after Christ should be in complete disaccord with the actions and opinions of the crowd and his model of piety should be Christ and no other.'*

Luther did indeed think that the reformers must bring the word of God to the people; he was to produce a translation of the Scriptures into German that was to become critical both for the development of German Protestantism and for that of the German language. Nevertheless, the élitism of the humanists was not to be irrelevant to the reformers, when the latter came to establish new churches.

The old clerical class was indeed to be abolished in the new reformed order, but the inaccessibility of the word of God to those without the learning needed to understand it was just as sure a guarantee of the continuance of a clerical order as the old Latin liturgy and dogma had been. Preaching the word of God required technical knowledge, although this was to be challenged by the sects that asserted the claims of the Spirit, and that held as Müntzer (see below) did that the common man could know the mind of Christ. To Lutherans and Calvinists this was unacceptable: university men were still to be able to find jobs in the Church.

'You bless yourself with holy water; what use is that if you fail to purify your heart from uncleanness? You venerate the saints, and love to touch their relics, but you pay no attention to their most precious example, that of a pure life. You contemplate with amazement the tunic and shroud of Christ, and you doze off when you are told what he said. You think yourselves fine folk, because you possess a relic of his cross. But that counts for nothing, if you don't store the mystery of the cross in your heart.' (Erasmus)

Reformed Churches

Luther turned out to be the precursor, and to some extent the model, for other reformers elsewhere in Europe. In Germany, naturally, his followers and allies among the learned and pious clergy were numerous, some of them to be important to him and to the development of his movement. In the Swiss Confederation, Huldrich Zwingli (1484–1531) was a similar rebel preacher, although initially not a monk in a religious order but a secular priest. In Zürich, from 1523 onwards. Zwingli launched a religious protest parallel to that of Luther, although conceived independently of Luther in most matters of dogma. Like Luther, Zwingli insisted that only faith can ensure the forgiveness of sin by God: as only the Holy Spirit can confer faith, so only the Holy Spirit can give forgiveness of sins.

Jean Calvin was the only one of the three major reformers to have been a classical and legal scholar, a humanist. He experienced religious conversion at some time around 1533–4, when he moved from being an orthodox university teacher in Paris to becoming an exiled reformer in Switzerland and Strasbourg. By 1535 Calvin was in Basle, where he wrote and in 1536 published his *Institutes of the Christian Religion*, and in 1541 he came to Geneva on the understanding that he would be one of the main leaders in establishing a new Christian polity in the city. Genevan politics denied his party absolute power there until 1555. The attempts to achieve a godly commonwealth in Geneva, 'the most perfect school of Christ that ever was on earth since the days of the apostles' (John Knox) were, almost inevitably, accompanied by something approaching totalitarian excess. It is easy to be unjust to Calvin, because of modern distaste for the closed community of the pious. But he was a man of the greatest possible literary, intellectual and spiritual gifts, and most remarkable of all for his vision of the absolute sovereignty of a merciful God.

© British Library, London, UK/Bridgeman Art Library

Left: Iconoclastic Calvinists smashed Catholic religious statuary to express their objection to the Catholic hegemony over Christianity.

The iconoclasm (or in their terms, condemnation of idolatry) that accompanied the reform was in its earlier stages a rather disorderly popular movement, which perhaps represented a sentimental smashing – in a literal sense – of a side of late medieval Catholicism that had been especially cherished by ordinary people. In its later stages it simply meant that churches were built or renovated bare of the statues and pictures of saints, and free too of institutions such as the rood screen that carried a representation of the crucified Christ. The abolition of chapels dedicated to particular saints automatically carried away their representations. Lutheranism did not in the least disdain the pictorial image: one of the most powerful propagandists of the Lutheran reform (although also a troubled one) was the artist Albrecht Dürer (1471–1528).

The Reform and the Princes

The reform of the Church upon the new principles enunciated by these men depended equally upon the lateral movement of a general disposition of Christians to accept their message, and upon the vertical movement of the acceptance of such reform by the princes and the oligarchies, without whose action such reform was going to be frustrated, in the end, by the Inquisitor and the executioner. The iron law of such matters was clearly demonstrated in the Italian peninsula, where in the absence of firm support from either France or Spain, which were disputing Italy between them, the existence of widespread evangelical sympathies, even in the heart of the papal court itself, never enabled a single evangelical government. Evangelical reform depended, in fact, upon political power.

© Private Collection/Bridgeman Art Library

Above: The Last Supper, *a woodcut published by the artist Albrecht Dürer, who was greatly influenced by Martin Luther.*

Above: The peasants' revolt in Germany was savagely put down and received no support from Luther. Religious reform did not at that time have any social dimension.

Although everyone was more or less vaguely aware that this was so, opinions on the matter differed both among the reformers and the princes. From the beginning Luther appealed to and depended upon the German princes and nobles, and when the Peasants' War (1524–5) appeared to suggest that his movement might acquire social revolutionary undertones, he immediately came down heavily on the side of law and order – although not without some moralistic criticism of the social role of the princes. Calvin was a lawyer and in most respects a realist, and he carefully dedicated his *Institutes of the Christian Religion* to Francis I of France. But when the French monarchy failed to respond, or responded only in a reserved and half-hearted way, Calvin steered his congregations in a direction that could resist oppressive authority.

Most of the European princes came from dynasties with centuries-old traditions of diplomacy and statecraft in managing and negotiating with the Church, and their legal systems were full of provisions for the eventualities of Church-State relations. The monarchs themselves were credited with some quasi-religious powers, that became especially evident in their coronation ceremonies. These had been the medieval foundations for the seventeenth-century theory of the Divine Right of Kings. At the minimum, the reform agitation changed the conditions on which the princes came to the negotiating table to bargain with the prelates, greatly to the disadvantage of the prelates.

The 'Catholic' monarchs had their own ecclesiastical agendas, most of them unfavourable to the Roman Court in one way or another. Henry VIII of England was just such a monarch. He was the author of a tract directed against the theology of Luther, and he ironically transmitted to his Protestant successors the papally-conferred title of 'Defender of the Faith'. He only moved into anti-papal opposition when his dynastic matrimonial needs required it; medieval history is full of Catholic kings who did exactly the same thing. The Catholic Emperor Charles V was for decades regarded by the popes as a dangerous enemy: he was crowned Holy Roman Emperor in 1530 by Pope Clement VII (pope 1523–34) three years after his troops had sacked Rome and driven the pope into hiding. In the century of Machiavelli it is not surprising that the Church politics of so many rulers should have been driven by cold-blooded calculation. Although this did not stop those same rulers – the Emperor Charles V and Francis I of France are notable examples, although Henry VIII of England was not far behind – from being convinced of their own fervent and pure Catholicism.

Some princes were genuinely convinced by the new reformers, although the extent to which Lutheranism was supported by Luther's Elector Frederick could only be described as active toleration; favourable legislation only occurred after Frederick's death in 1525. In the early 1530s, after the Protestant princes had registered their 'Protest' in the Diet of 1529, the Protestant princes and towns joined in the political alliance of the League of Schmalkald, a league in which the germ of later religious war was located. In Scandinavia Gustav Vasa of Sweden (1496–1560) carried out a reformation whose aims were almost as political as those of the reformation sponsored by Henry VIII of England. Henry VIII's à la carte view of Church reform, by which he specified in a very conservative spirit the degree of Protestantism to be allowed to the reforming clergy, may be said to have embodied the politically controlled reform of the princes.

Above: Francis I (1494–1547) of France, a pragmatic Catholic and a cruel persecutor of Protestants.

Reform in the Roman Communion

Although the pressures for a 'reform in head and members' of the Catholic Church appeared to have been frustrated by the tame and half-hearted Fifth Lateran Council, the widespread demand for a Catholic reform had not gone away. The big papal problem remained what it had been ever since the birth of the 'conciliar' movement at the end of the fourteenth century: that the popes feared above all things that an 'oecumenical council', which claimed divine inspiration like that of the first seven (or on another reckoning eight) oecumenical councils of the ancient world, might be politically used to enslave the Church. This was not necessarily a politicized view of the Church, although it was the view of men to whom political considerations were always present.

There were many Catholic bishops and holy men whose piety and good faith in the matter of reform were beyond doubt, and whose abilities as humanists and scholars of Christian history and theology were not inferior to those of the reformers. Indeed, Erasmus himself, who wrote against Luther on free will, and spent his last days between Catholic Freiburg and Protestant Basle, may be said to have belonged to the second of these categories, and to have gained from it only the lasting distaste of the Protestant reformers and the lasting distrust of Catholic orthodoxy.

Right: An Allegory of the Reformation, *painted between 1568–71. Henry VIII, who moved from Catholicism to Protestantism to suit his own dynastic agenda, is seen on his death-bed handing on his work to the future Edward VI, seated on the throne. Popery is shown in a state of collapse.*

Above: Charles V of Hapsburg marching into Bologna for his coronation as Holy Roman Emperor. Charles was considered an enemy of the papacy – his troops had sacked Rome – but such was his political ascendance that he was crowned by Pope Clement VII.

Right: A contemporary copper engraving of the interior of the cathedral at Trent (Trento) with a sitting of the Council of Trent in session.

Below: Cardinal Reginald Pole (1500–58), a violent anti-Protestant, clashed with Henry VIII but was appointed Archbishop of Canterbury by the Catholic Mary I.

The choice of Trent (modern Trento), a bishopric within the Holy Roman Empire, but within geographical reach of what is now Italy, for the first sessions of a council of Catholic reformation (1545–7), already showed the concessions that the popes had been forced to make to the feared Empire. In the earlier sessions the Council of Trent was under strong German pressure to make doctrinal concessions to the Lutherans, which it resisted, so that the 'Tridentine' definitions on justification and grace (meaning, those made at Trent) allowed human merit and human free will as elements in salvation, and asserted that inner sanctification accompanies the forgiveness that Christ's salvation procures for man. The idea that justifying faith, which assures the believer of redemption, is nothing other than trust in the divine mercy that remits sins for Christ's sake was anathematized. One of the three papal cardinals to preside was the English Cardinal Pole (1500–58) who, in spite of the reputation for repression that he later acquired in his own country, was in papal terms counted as a closet evangelical. At the time of his death the Inquisition had assembled a thick and hostile dossier on his career.

Fearful of more Imperial and Lutheran pressure, Pope Paul III (pope from 1534–49) transferred the council from Trent to papal territory in Bologna: it was then prorogued, and reopened in Trent in 1551, and attended by Protestant delegates. This was the only attempt made after the Protestant Schism to achieve reunion, and it failed. In spite of the diplomatic support given to the Protestants by the emperor, who wanted a compromise to avert further civil war in Germany, theological definition had become too sharp on either side, and the attempt was abandoned, the council again prorogued.

Ignatius Loyola (1491–1556), the founder of the Company of Jesus, secured the favour of Paul III in Rome in 1538, and his new religious order received papal approval in 1540. Ignatius (born Iñigo) came from the minor nobility of the Basque country of Navarre; he had been converted while convalescing from war wounds in 1521–2. He brought to the apostolate the warrior's fervour and temperament, and the greatest ability as leader and administrator, but he had also, as the English Catholic poet Francis Thompson remarked, a great belief in that gentlemanly and soldier-like word, 'accommodate' that his followers were in the end to give a theological dimension.

The devotion that he preached was an affective piety, that was given a systematic character by the required practice of his spiritual 'exercises', in which the aspirant visualized the conflict of good and evil as a sort of sacred dramatic performance of the mind. He was the general of a new force of holy troops, whose loyalty went first absolutely to the pope, and then to the general of the spiritual order. It was an élitist concept of a small force of officers, especially educated and prepared, who were at the absolute disposal of the head of the Roman Church. The order reflected humanist ideas on élitist education, and also humanist distaste for the traditional formulae for the religious life, of regular recitation of the holy offices in choir. The constitution of the order was so deeply pondered that it did not get papal approval until two years after the death of Ignatius.

The final and decisive sessions of the council, recalled once more to Trent in 1562, are those that most confirm the title of 'Counter-Reformation' that was applied to the Catholic reform movement some three centuries after it had taken place. When the Council of Trent finally ended in January 1564, what had been achieved was to some extent a renewal of Catholic hearts and minds, but always with an eye to Protestant opposition (for example, in the repudiation of Protestant iconoclasm), and always with the intention of reinforcing the central control of Rome. So that even the decrees that were intended to renew the powers of bishops over their own dioceses were counterbalanced by others that reinforced papal authority.

The Sects

The question of authority in Protestant churches was just as central as in Catholicism, although posed in a different way. There were enormous variations in the way that Protestant congregations were governed, but broadly speaking they can be divided into those in which authority was in some way centralized – often, but not always, associated with princely power – and those in which it was not. The biggest problems for mainstream Protestantism arose from the growth of splinter movements that usually assembled around individual prophets who claimed divine inspiration, though there were also particular doctrines such as Anabaptism that spread very widely. All these were apostles of the gathered Church, the visible group of saved believers. Their saved condition was emphasized often by re-baptism (hence Anabaptism), a rite bitterly condemned by all the main reformers, but perhaps most of all by Calvin. Anabaptism proclaimed a sort of inner conversion that in a way guaranteed salvation, but that required the believer to continue to show that he or she was sanctified.

The model for sectarian extremism was the Anabaptist Thomas Müntzer (c.1490–1525), a former Catholic priest turned Lutheran, who then became convinced of the revelation vouchsafed him by the Holy Spirit. Müntzer was formidable in his belief that the elect of God were justified in using violence to further their cause. He saw himself as a 'second Daniel, who will lead his people like Moses', and at the time of the Peasants' War he set up a tiny theocratic rule in the little town of Mühlhausen in Thuringia. Unsurprisingly the nobles suppressed his regime in blood. But Anabaptism did not die with him, and small groups survived in many places, in spite of the most fearful and barbaric treatment of its advocates almost everywhere.

Above: The massacre of St Bartholomew's Day shown in a sixteenth-century German woodcut. At the instigation of Catherine de Medici, almost 25,000 Protestant Huguenots were slaughtered in Paris between 24 August and 17 September 1572. The slaughter went on outside Paris until 3 October, and Catherine de Medici was congratulated by the pope.

The Wars of Religion

By the late sixteenth century it had become quite clear that whatever Protestantism stood for, it did not stand for toleration. The sort of élitist toleration that characterized some humanists, and the closet Protestants in Catholic lands – Nicodemists, as Calvin called them (from Nicodemus, who came to Jesus by night for fear of the Jews) – had no future at all in European power politics. The Erasmian eirenic formula of 'agree quickly and discuss little' was adopted by no one. On the Catholic side there was equal intolerance. The setting up of the Roman Inquisition and of the Roman Index of prohibited books, and institution of the Jesuits in mid-century, spoke clearly of what was to come. The one attempt to meet and reunite with the Protestants at Trent had broken down almost as soon as it began.

From the 1530s onwards German Protestantism had led to political alliances of the princes. The victory of the Emperor Charles V over the principal Protestant alliance in the war of the League of Schmalkald in 1547 brought no permanent political solution. In France, a very large and powerful faction of the nobility had passed to Protestantism. Although there was widespread desire at the top of the French monarchy to work out some kind of compromise with this very powerful group, factional violence and religious zeal in the end forbade it. France drifted towards civil war just as Germany had already done. In the 1560s what had originally been French Protestant churches started to become also paramilitary organizations. There were temporary peace arrangements for a limited toleration of Protestantism, and it was certainly the main aim of the government to avoid maximum confrontation if it could, but this policy broke down under factional pressure, and there was a paroxysm of violence in the massacre of St Bartholomew's Day in Paris (1572) and the further bloodletting that followed elsewhere.

The religious splits forced themselves into every corner of European life, and became identified with national quarrels and rebellions such as those of the Dutch Netherlands against Spain. Protestant and Catholic powers allowed their foreign policies to become to some extent dominated by religious agendas. Christendom had in many respects broken down, although it could still sometimes unite against the Turks.

1 E. F. Jacob, *Essays in the Conciliar Epoch* (Manchester, 1943).

Left: An Anti-Catholic allegory depicting Stephen Gardiner, Bishop of Winchester. Gardiner had been made bishop by Henry VIII, imprisoned by Edward VI and restored by Mary I, when he became a scourge of Protestantism. Here he is shown, with other Catholic priests, in wolf's clothing. Protestants are shown as the lambs of God, slain by the Catholics.

6

New Worlds and Old

The first Puritan settlement on the north-eastern coast of North America arose out of the persecution of the Calvinist groups of God's elect by the established Anglican Church of England. Many of the tiny group that sailed in the *Mayflower* to what they named Plymouth in Cape Cod Bay in 1620 had already been in exile for several years in Holland before they left for America. They had embarked with the intention of settling in northern Virginia, but the Atlantic winds decided otherwise. The second and much larger emigration of 1630, which settled a few miles north in Boston, came with a royal charter granted to the Company of Massachusetts Bay in New England; the scale and speed of its growth were to be much greater than those of the little church of Plymouth.

Signature of Col. Thomas Knolton, of Ashford, who was killed near New York, Sept. 1776. (*See page* 419.)

[Portrait of John Winthrop, first Governor of Connecticut under the Charter, copied from an engraving in Trumbull's History of Connecticut, with a fac simile of his hand writing.]

John Winthrop, F. R. S., Governor of Connecticut, the eldest son of John Winthrop, the first Governor of Massachusetts, was born at Groton, in England, in 1605. He was educated at the University of Dublin, and afterwards traveled into France, Hol-

Above: John Winthrop (1588-1649) the first governor of the second Puritan settlement at Massachusetts Bay.

Both groups had a sense of historic destiny. William Bradford (1589–1657), the leader and governor of the Plymouth colony, wrote after 1647 that 'as one small candle may light a thousand, so the light here kindled hath shone to many, yea in some sort to our whole [English] nation.' John Winthrop (1588–1649), the leader and governor of the second (Massachusetts Bay) settlement, said to his congregation at its beginning that 'We must consider that we shall be as a city upon a hill, the eyes of all people are upon us.'

Zion in the Wilderness

The whole enterprise at this stage marked only the movement of a few thousand Congregationalist Calvinists to a bleak American wilderness – a wilderness that after a score of years had reduced some of the original clerical leaders to something not far off despair, and the desire, which they could not satisfy, to go home to England. But it was marked also by the imagination and energy that were to

Left: The first Puritan settlers in America make landfall from the Mayflower *on 11 December 1620.*

Above: The Peaceable Kingdom *(1833) by Quaker artist Edward Hicks. This utopian vision shows humans and animals living together under one God in the innocent state enjoyed before the Fall. In the background, true to Quaker principles, new settlers are discoursing amicably with the indigenous inhabitants.*

create in the end a widespread national belief in 'one nation under God'. Or this was how things were to seem by the nineteenth century, even if, at the time of its foundation in the eighteenth century, the American nation was already very distant from sectarian unity, and was under notoriously Enlightened – although Deist – leadership.

The Puritans were quite late among those who came to the Americas bearing a passionate Christian committment, and the sense of taking the path marked by God for Christian people to walk in. Almost a century earlier, in 1523, the twelve Franciscans who were to accompany the military force for the conquest of Central America by Hernando Cortés had been appointed by their general with the message that the world was rapidly nearing its end, and that they went to America like the son who worked at the eleventh hour in the lord's vineyard (Matt. 21: 30–31).[1]

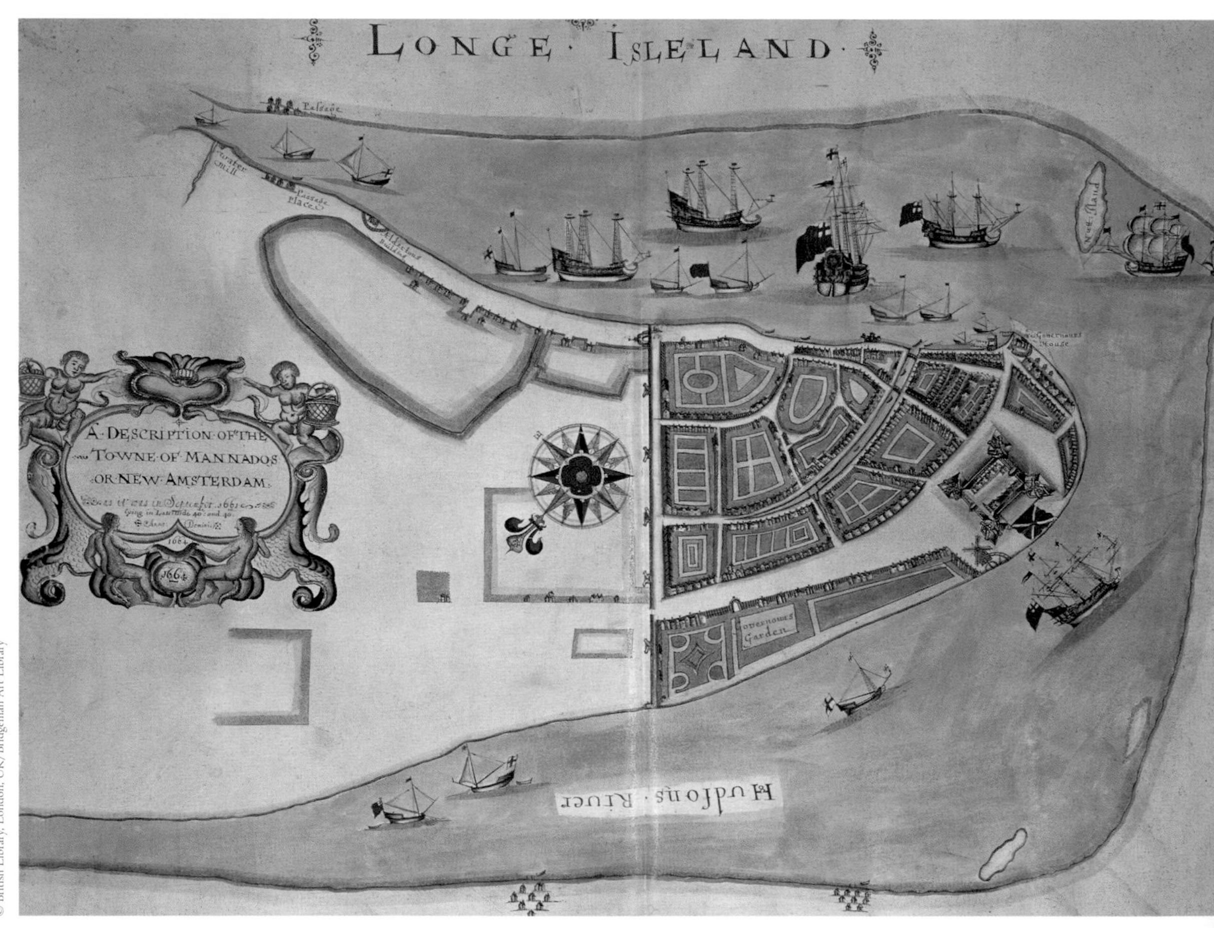

Right: An early map of New Amsterdam (later New York) showing Manhattan, Long Island and the Hudson River. Dutch Protestants were the first to settle in this area.

By the early seventeenth century, Catholic settlements and missions in the Americas had become important and populous in a way that made the tiny Puritan settlement in the north-east look for a very long time to be totally insignificant. And, indeed, its significance comes from its place in the American national myth, not from its place in the history of Christianity. The Catholic American world ran from Peru and Brazil in the south through Central America to New Mexico and Florida; in the north it was strong in French Canada (where Huguenots had also been represented). The Christian mission to the Native

Americans, which the Puritans had scarcely launched by mid-century, was in Catholic North America already significant, though slow in achieving its aims. There were also Dutch Protestant settlements on the Hudson and the Delaware, Swedish ones elsewhere. The English Anglican settlement in Virginia (originally begun in 1607–09) had provided the administrative pattern for the later Massachusetts venture.

At the heart of Puritanism lay the denial of episcopacy; the whole institution was seen as a main source of impurity in the Church. No bishops were recognized in Puritan America of the north-east. Anglicanism had been from the beginning established in Virginia, in the south, although there were no resident bishops there or elsewhere in British America during the whole colonial period. Nor was there a resident Catholic bishop for the Catholics who were present in Maryland after 1634. In Latin and French America, by contrast, bishops were ubiquitous.

Left: A map of Virginia, the land settled by the Anglicans, showing Chief Powhatan on the left. He was the father of Pocahontas, the princess who embraced Christianity, was baptized as Rebecca, and married the Englishman John Rolfe.

The Fellowship of the Elect

American Congregationalism was in the first and most important period of its existence no more tolerant than the European churches from which it sprang. The minister Nathaniel Ward (1579–1652), who was part of the original leadership, wrote that: 'He that is willing to tolerate any Religion, or any discrepant way of Religion, besides his own, unless it be in matters merely indifferent, either doubts of his own, or is not sincere in it.'

In spite of asserting the priority of the gathered congregation of the saved, the fellowship of saints, Calvinist doctrine as understood by the early American Puritans kept a certain residual priestly element. Godly preachers meant trained preachers: in 1636, Harvard University was founded to ensure a supply of men to preach God's word. The minister's relationship with the flock he served was thought of as depending on a covenant with the congregation.

The critical issues arose early, with the appearance of vocal and articulate opposition to the ministers within their congregations. The minister's task was to preach the word of God so as be a means of grace: to do this he must be 'inwardly taught by the spiritual Schoolmaster the Holy Ghost'.[2] On the whole the ministers themselves asserted that the promise of grace could not depend upon empty works, but must be fulfilled by the promptings of the spirit. There was a successful movement to compel the members of the congregation to testify or 'relate' about their own conversions – no theoretical matter, since the colonists had no voting rights as citizens unless they were recognized as members of the church congregation.

The only long-term answer to disquiet among the congregations was to satisfy their discontents, which to some extent was done by the gloomy means of 'labouring for a sense of sin and misery' among them. They could not satisfy those who asserted the claims of spiritual inspiration. The socially well-connected Anne Hutchinson (c. 1590–1643) said that the ministers had only a legalistic way of preparing their flocks for conversion, and preached a doctrine of salvation through works. The clergy were outraged, and labelled her 'Antinomian', that taken literally meant she denied that Christians live under a moral law. The charge was untrue, but her emphasis on the inspiration of the free spirit was not unlike the things that the Quakers were to be saying in a few years. The ministers resorted, in 1637, to the very traditionalist way of calling a synod that banished her from the community; she went to Rhode Island and then to Rye, north of New York, where she was killed by hostile Native Americans.

The coming parliamentary victory in England would place the church settlement in New England in some doubt, because the new settlement in Republican England could have threatened that across the Atlantic – which had never for a moment been cited in the homeland as a possible model. The 'Cambridge Platform' that the New England congregations adopted in 1648 went along with the Parliament-dominated Westminster Confession of faith of 1646, and made significant concessions to the authority of church ministers.

New England was never a theocracy. Government under the royal charter rested with the governor and his ten officers, who had judicial powers, and possessed also a right of veto over the General Court to which all freemen belonged. The franchise rested in Massachusetts with the congregations, because membership of the General Court depended on being recognized as belonging to a congregation. When the immigrants started to include many who were not in any way saints, the absence of godliness meant exclusion from the congregation, and consequently the inability to exercise free-citizen rights. The clergy, because the material existence of the churches depended upon favourable legislation, exerted their influence in favour of the governor.

In their relations with the Native Americans, the northern colonists did not have the military power to make the forced conversions that had characterized the evangelization of Latin America. Preaching to the Indians was seen by a few of the Puritan ministers as an urgent religious duty; the majority took a different view, perhaps most of all because of the language difficulties, but also from an attitude towards the closed number of the elect that went far back into medieval Christianity. One or two learned Native American languages, and John Eliot (1604–90) made a translation of the Bible into Algonquian that he published in 1663, and distributed to learned colleges on his subsequent fund-raising trip, in England, for the Society for the Propagation of the Gospel in New England. The frontier allowed a great deal of trading, and some co-operation with Native Americans, but there were also the Indian Wars.

Troubles and Dissent in the New England Society of Saints

In England, baptism was automatically administered to the child of any Anglican Christian. In New England this had ceased to be so, because of the obligation to 'relate' conversion in order to claim membership of a congregation. By mid-century, approaching half the population were not in the full sense members of a church (although the legal obligation of church attendance continued to affect everyone), and the churches faced the classical threat to the gathered churches, of decline towards insignificance. The answer they offered was the so-called half-way covenant, that in the end was to cause a return to automatic baptism of the children of church members.

Below: Many religious settlers felt bound to preach Christianity to the inhabitants of their new home, but this was not always welcomed. Here three Jesuits are martyred by hostile Native Americans.

In the period in which the initial evangelical impulse was on the decline, the New England churches met the full impact of the sects that claimed the inspiration of the spirit as a mandate for their doctrines. The Baptists had been treated by Jean Calvin as 'Catabaptists, who deny that we have been duly baptized because we were baptized by impious and idolatrous men'. Calvin had denounced the 'follies' of adult rebaptism, because he maintained baptism to be not of man but of God, no matter who administers it, and in Geneva he had backed up this denial with persecution.

The Congregational ministers in New England initially harassed the Baptists with fines, imprisonment, disenfranchisement, the usual array of penalties. But after the Restoration in England, in 1660, and the proclamation of toleration for Protestants by the Restoration government, it proved impossible to continue with proscription of Baptists. Encouraged by English Anglicans, the colony slid quietly towards toleration.

The Quakers were treated by everyone as a different matter. They were children of the English Civil War, in that their origins lay in the peak period of the claims to proclaim doctrine by inspiration of the spirit, by divine 'openings' in the parlance of their leader, George Fox (1625–91), of a sort that were rife among the Independents. Though certainly not Ranters, who were spiritual anarchists, the Quakers had grown in the same environment, and quite a lot of the ferocious distrust and hostility they aroused came from their being, after the Restoration of the monarchy, the solitary and conspicuous survivors in England of the alarming religious sects of the early times of the Commonwealth.

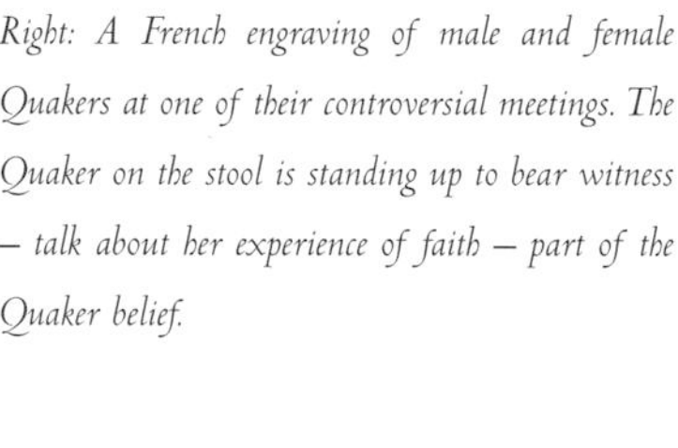

Right: A French engraving of male and female Quakers at one of their controversial meetings. The Quaker on the stool is standing up to bear witness – talk about her experience of faith – part of the Quaker belief.

The toleration shown in England for Baptists and Presbyterians (the latter of whom had been of critical importance in the English Church settlement of the Commonwealth period) did not extend to Quakers, in spite of the immensely careful efforts of Quakers to give testimony without giving scandal. They went deliberately against the great shibboleth of the *ancien régime*, the outward respect for 'degree' and social order. Refusal to doff a hat or make a reverence, or to address people by their correct title, were profoundly shocking to seventeenth-century people, and the more so if the discourtesies proceeded from a woman, as in the Quaker case they often did. The Commonwealth government had never, in fact, shown itself notably favourable to Quakers. Oliver Cromwell had been willing to ride alongside the Quaker leader, George Fox, in Hyde Park, but his magistrates were quite willing to put both Fox and his followers into prison.

In New England the persecutions of Quakers were in some respects more severe than those in England. The more usual punishments were flogging, branding, or banishment, which meant Quakers fled to a more tolerant Rhode Island, or to part-Catholic Maryland. But the Quaker missionary spirit, especially among women, that took them to plead their cause with the pope and the Great Turk (the Ottoman sultan), was not going to be discouraged in the Americas. Between 1659 and 1661 four Quakers, including a woman, were executed in Boston for returning to the colony after their banishment. When George Fox came to North America in 1672–3 he went to Virginia, to North Carolina, to Maryland, but, although he attended the yearly meeting of the Friends (as the Quakers were and are called) of New England, it took place in non-hostile Rhode Island, and not in Massachusetts. In its punitive intolerance the Congregationalist establishment in New England showed that it belonged to an earlier world of rigid religious conformism, which had been weakened even in Restoration England, and which became very fragile in North America. It was to make a final, and rather tragic, intolerant gesture.

There were pressures on the colonist communities that excuse their tendency to panic, notably the danger and destruction of the Indian Wars of the 1670s. In 1692 there was a major witchcraft panic in the village of Salem just north of Boston, which led to the execution of nineteen suspects and the judicial torture to death of a twentieth. The episode has seemed especially superstitious and disgraceful to generations that have come to expect enlightenment to be conferred on people who breathe North American air; in Europe, where witch-hunts had been endemic from the fourteenth to seventeenth centuries, it would have seemed rather late in the day for such things, but not unexpected in a remote province.

The Quakers were to return in force to North America in a context that meant that they were to become big influences in the drift towards toleration and religious pluralism. This major experiment was born of old-fashioned political patronage and favouritism received from a Catholic prince. William Penn (1644–1718) was the son of an admiral to whom the Duke of York had become indebted. Penn, who had been converted to Quakerism in 1667, received the royal grant of the huge tract of land west of the River Delaware that became Pennsylvania. To this immense domain came at his invitation not only Quakers but also Baptists, principally Mennonites, from German and Dutch-speaking lands in continental Europe. The frame of government that Penn set out for the colony in 1682 gave toleration to all Christian groups that worshipped a single God, and promised that no one would be compelled to frequent or maintain a place of worship 'contrary to his mind'. This is no small matter if we think not only of the intolerance of Massachusetts, but also of the preservation of the death penalty in Maryland for those who blasphemed or denied the Trinity. The drift towards religious multiplicity in the American colonies owed a great deal to Penn.

Above: An engraving visualizing one of the 'Witches of Salem' terrorizing young girls. The hysterical witch-hunting episode ended in the hanging of nineteen people.

Below: Matthew Hopkins, the Witchfinder General, looking for clues. Hopkins was appointed in 1644 during the witch-fearing craze that swept Cromwellian England in the seventeenth century. Over 100 women were hanged as a result of his actions, but he was allegedly himself hanged as a witch in 1647.

Right: A Currier & Ives print showing the Quaker William Penn negotiating a peaceful treaty in 1661 with the Native American inhabitants of what became known as Pennsylvania.

Catholicism and American Mission

No greater contrast could exist than between the shifting world of North American Protestantism, which lived upon what was literally a moving frontier, and the hierarchic perspectives of Catholicism from south to north of the Americas. Nevertheless, the resemblances between the two apparently opposed worlds are more than might at first sight be supposed, especially as they concern the rights of indigenous Americans.

The origins of the concern of the Roman Church with the missionary field of newly-discovered overseas lands lay in the West African voyages of the Portuguese in the mid-fifteenth century. The Portuguese were authorized by the popes to rule specific named areas of lands conquered south of the Sahara, with the obligation to evangelize the populations. This did not remain a dead letter: Portuguese-imported Christianity was already a powerful influence in the African kingdom of the Congo, before Columbus sailed to America.

When the famous division of the New World between Portugal and Spain was made by Pope Alexander VI in 1493, the pope was not operating in a void, but applying some of the principles of the earlier papal concessions to help Spain and Portugal to modify an earlier treaty of 1479–80. The earlier agreement had been concerned with West Africa, but some of its clauses seemed applicable to the new Atlantic world after the discoveries of Columbus in 1492.

From the start it looked as though conversion of the new subject peoples would be easy. What their rights were to be was a different matter, though not one to which Christian missionaries were indifferent. At a very early stage – from the time of their indignation in the early fifteenth century at the horrible way in which the indigenous inhabitants of the Canary Islands were being treated – some

Left: A bronze from Benin showing a Portuguese soldier, complete with what was at the time a state-of-the-art matchlock rifle. Portugal dominated the colonization and Christianization of West Africa, of which Benin is a part.

Above: An Aztec vision of Hernando Cortés, the treacherous Spanish conquistador believed by the Aztecs to be an embodiment of their god Quetzlcoatl. His relative size in the image indicates his significance.

of the missionaries protested. Unhappily, when their protests went to the Church authorities in Europe, the reasoning of power politics intruded upon the reasoning of the Gospel.

The material interests at stake in the conquest of the Americas were huge, but religious values were not absent from Spanish or Portuguese royal policies. Because the reconquest of the Iberian peninsula provided the model for Portugese and Spanish colonialism in the New World, the popes gave the Iberian kings enormous rights over the colonial churches. The original 'Requirement' issued by the Castilian government to guide colonial policy did try to reserve some rights of peaceful possession to the indigenous inhabitants, provided that they submitted peacefully – unfortunately, it was almost impossible for the 'requirements' to be made known to them before the guns opened fire. And it was acknowledged that conversion had to be made freely and without duress – an important matter, especially because of the dire penalties imposed by the Inquisition for so-called apostasy.

The American conquests were made by a military culture that in the Iberian wars had acquired a tradition of political and religious domination, and which was not in the least ashamed of its lust for booty. They thought of themselves in the New World as entering a sort of cultural vacuum, occupied by barbarians who did not possess the coherence and aggressiveness of Islam. Hernando Cortés, the conqueror of the Aztecs, had assured the Aztec King Montezuma, shortly before he took and executed him, of the Christian principle that all men are brothers.

Right: The dead bodies of Montezuma, the Aztec king, and his courtier Itzquzuhtzin are cast into the sea by the conquering Spaniards. Cortés had assured Montezuma of the brotherhood of man, but then had him executed.

Among the three groups, the conquistadores, the royal officials who were supposed to supervise them, and the religious – mostly friars, for a long time – who were to undertake the missions, each pursued rather different aims. But it was the first of these who ultimately called the tune, and preferred that the Americans should live as the slaves of Christian folk, rather than as 'free beasts'. It was the victory of the principles of conquest and naked exploitation.

Slavery was never accepted by the churchmen as being the inevitable lot of the conquered in the new lands, and to some extent the Spanish kings backed them up, although the way in which slavery was cloaked under enserfment was never taken too seriously. By the mid-sixteenth century some of the religious missionaries in Latin America had become very conscious of the terrible injustice done to the conquered peoples, part of which had been the gratuitous supposition that they had possessed no worthwhile identity and culture of their own. The missionaries began to construct, belatedly, ethnographic descriptions of some of the indigenous American cultures that recognized their independent existence.

As had happened centuries earlier in Europe, the missionary churches in the Americas had their mass conversions, but had to accept some compromises with the beliefs and cultures of the converted peoples. A notable example is the appearance of the Virgin of Guadalupe, north of Mexico City. It was reported in 1638 that a poor Indian, Juan Diego, had been told by the Virgin to take flowers to the Bishop of Mexico. He gathered the flowers in his cape, made of cactus fibre, and when he opened it to offer them, a miraculous image of the Virgin was found to have been imprinted upon the cape. The image of Guadalupe (the name was borrowed from a shrine dedicated to the Virgin in Spain) came from the Aztec shrine of Tepeyac, on the Guadalupe sierra. It was thus a product of the

Above: After the conquest of Mexico by Cortés (1519-21), the Catholic Church made many converts.

Left: A picture catechism used as a teaching aid by Catholic missionaries to the Americas. Catholic missions were established before the arrival of the Puritans.

Below: Native South Americans are used as slave labour to build the foundations of the cathedral in Mexico City. The Catholic conquistadors claimed to believe that Americans were better off living as 'slaves of Christian folk rather than free beasts'.

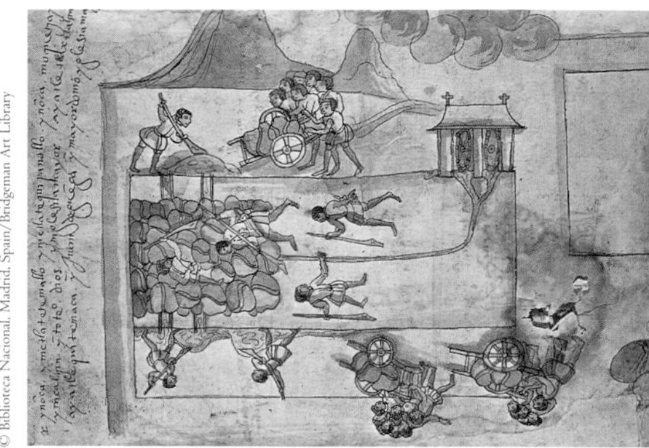

© Museo de America, Madrid, Spain/Bridgeman Art Library

Right: The Virgin of Guadaloupe, an image of the coalescence between Catholic iconography, Native American artistry and perhaps also Aztec pre-Christian tradition.

indigenous culture, even if it conformed to the European pattern of images made to honour the immaculate conception of Mary. Although reported in 1638, the miraculous appearance of the image was said to have occurred over a century earlier, which perhaps indicates that there had been a long resistance among the clergy to what was known to have been a heathen borrowing, until the reluctance was overcome by a more established Creole culture, a century later.

One or two of the Latin American clergy began to protest loudly in Europe at the magnitude of the injustices that had been done in the New World. The most widely known and influential protest was that of Bishop Bartolomé de las Casas (1484–1566), who published his account of the destruction of the 'Western Indies' in the mid-sixteenth century. De las Casas was well informed about the life and history of Central America (he was a Mexican bishop), and about South America as far south as Peru. He denounced the crimes of colonial rule in the Americas, where he arrived in 1502, in no uncertain terms, and did in fact succeed in influencing the colonial policies enunciated in Spain, although his influence on the ground in Central America was more limited. His polemic was translated and republished by the Protestants, with appropriate illustrations of the atrocities, on several occasions, although without any visible effect on the colonial policies of Protestant powers. De las Casas set a pattern for the conscientious modern defence of the rights of indigenous American peoples that has lasted into our own times, and the modern champions of conscience have included a bishop of his own diocese, Chiapas, in south Mexico. Defence of the rights of indigenous peoples has claimed at least a couple of bishop-martyrs in the present century.

Above: Illustration from Bishop Bartolomé de las Casas' Destruction of the Western Indies *showing the cruelties of colonial rule.*

In Paraguay, from the beginning of the seventeenth century until nearing the end of the eighteenth, there was a development quite different from anything else in America, that of a colony founded and run by the Christian priesthood. The Jesuit Order was so tightly disciplined, and consisted of such a dedicated band of men, that it was able to organize the population, who voluntarily accepted inclusion into what was virtually a huge religious community. Jesuit influence on the Catholic colonial powers was great enough to persuade them to accept this exceptional religious intrusion into the heart of the colonial world, that became a zone over which the Catholic princes had only the most shadowy control. Like the Massachusetts community, it was a body run by the saints, but, unlike it, the layfolk of the enterprise were Native Americans.

Below: Seventeenth-century painting of a Jesuit priest at work in India.

The Missions to the Ancient Cultures of Asia

In Asia the same pattern as in America of a colonial European domination with economic, political and religious aspects tended to impose itself, although its development took place over a very much longer period, and when the missionaries came into contact with the ancient cultures of China and Japan they were compelled to assume very different attitudes. There was also, in Asia, much missionary action that was directly controlled from the Catholic centre in Rome: the phenomenon of a colonial Church virtually granted to the colonial power was not the prevalent one. From 1622 there was a central agency for missions in Rome, called the De Propaganda Fide.

In Asia the Jesuits were, again, immensely important. The Portuguese were the key carriers by sea and the key colonizers. In India they did not come to lands entirely without Christ. There was a more than millennial history of Christianity in India when the Portuguese took their guns, troops

Above: Shah Jahangir, the third Moghul emperor known as the Conqueror of the World, holding a picture of the Madonna.

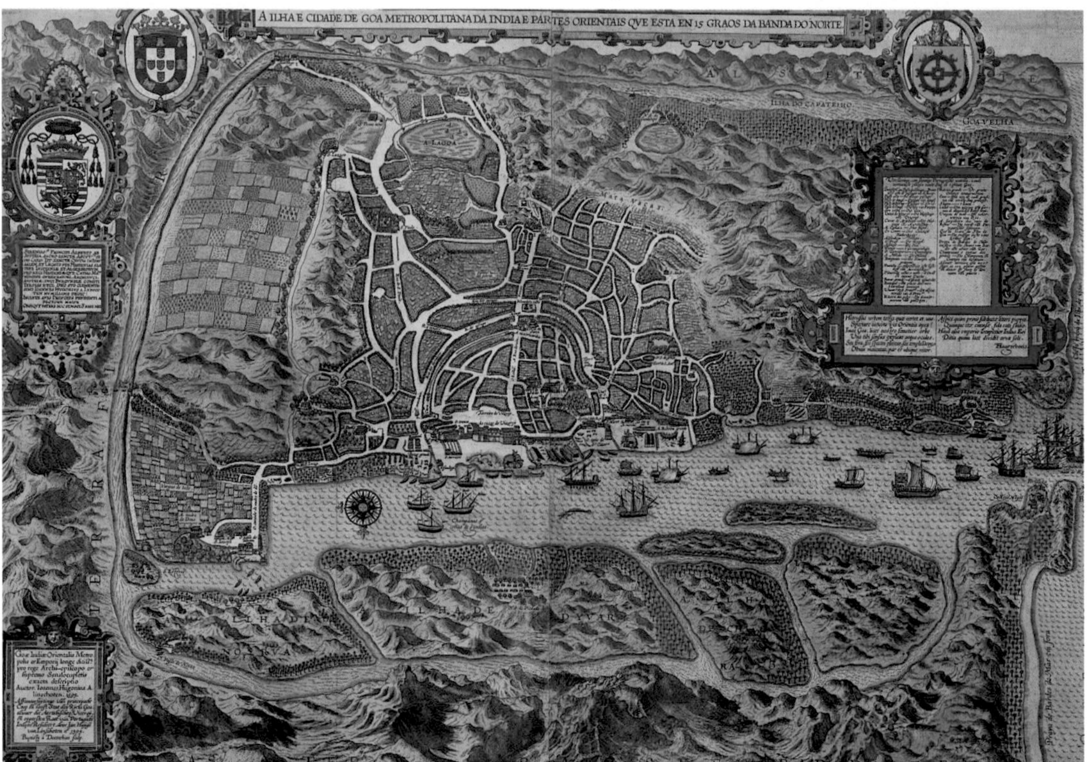

Right: A map of the city and port of Goa engraved by Johannes Doetechum. Goa was the Portuguese jumping-off point for the East, Japan in particular.

Above: A nineteenth-century engraving of the Basque-born Jesuit Francis Xavier (1506–52), known as the 'Apostle of the Indies'. In 1542, he was sent by John III of Portugal to be a missionary to the Portuguese colony of Goa, where he had great success.

and traders there – in no inconsiderable numbers – to establish 'factories' or trading posts in south India from the early sixteenth century. To a large extent the Portuguese were welcomed, but subsequently the Syriac and Eastern (believed by the Latin clergy to be Nestorian) religious culture of the native Indian Christians was unacceptable to the Portuguese, just as the bullying and interfering habits of the Portuguese priests disturbed the Indians.

It was a marriage, but a somewhat unhappy one. The 'Thomas Christians' of India had traditions that were supposed to go back to the sojourn of the apostle Thomas in India, and that certainly could have begun in the second and third centuries. Their earlier allegiance had been to the Syriac patriarch of Babylon. At the end of the sixteenth century, after the death of their last native metropolitan, the tensions between the Malabar native Christians and the Portuguese hierarchy came to a head. In 1599 an armed clash was narrowly avoided, and papal authority 'finally' reimposed – although sporadic religious resistance continued for centuries.

From Goa, the main Portuguese naval base in India, the Jesuits could embark for the Far East. St Francis Xavier (1506–52), one of the companions of Ignatius Loyola, was first in Goa in 1542, then left with two Jesuit companions and a solitary Japanese Christian convert, for Japan in 1549. The feudal samurai, engaged in internecine warfare, were not indisposed to welcoming people who might bring foreign aid and important technical military skills. Western and southern Japan saw a quite rapid growth of Christianity between 1551 and 1587, supported by a number of important nobles.

There was in the early 1580s, shortly before the beginning of the persecutions, a significant modification of cultural policy by the Jesuit leadership, that was to have more important results in

China than in Japan. The policy in India had been to fight the local indigenous Christian traditions so as to leave room for a centralized and papalist religious policy. But in the later period it was decided – although already too late – to adopt a policy that left far more religious room to the language and culture of the Japanese than the missionaries had formerly allowed.

However, the Japanese mission was unstable, principally because it depended on the goodwill of the Japanese warrior class. Perhaps because of fear of the colonial ambitions of the Spaniards (by now firmly established in the Philippines), perhaps because of the quarrels of foreign trade interests and the intervention of Dutch and English Protestants, but also because of purely internal Japanese political factors, the samurai began at the end of the penultimate decade of the century to reject and to proscribe the Christians. Twenty-six Christians were martyred at Nagasaki in 1597, and in 1614 the powerful shogun Ieyasu issued an edict which alleged that the Christians were conspiring to impose their religion and to seize power in the land. Finally, after a failed Christian peasant revolt in the island of Kyushu, a very large number of Christians were executed for rebellion or martyred for their religion (often by being crucified and left in the shallows of the inshore waters to die), and Christianity became for centuries in Japan a tiny underground sect professed only by a very few in a completely clandestine form. The persecutions are the setting for Shusaka Endo's tragic novel, *Silence*. Buddhist culture had won.

The fate of the Catholic mission in China was very different. The Chinese mission was launched by a gifted Italian Jesuit, Matteo Ricci (1552–1610), whose work had been enabled by the setting up of a special Jesuit training establishment for the Chinese mission in the Portuguese island factory of Macao. Ricci and another Jesuit managed to obtain admission to a city near Canton in 1583, and they remained there for some years, studying the classical language and the culture of China.

Above: A lacquer screen showing the arrival of the Portuguese Jesuits in Japan. Note how tall the Europeans are.

Below: A seventeenth-century engraved map of China, showing Matteo Ricci on the left.

Ricci divined that the mental and social approaches of Western humanism had a great deal in common with the equally élitist culture of China, and in effect he pursued the analogy further, by realizing that the Chinese imperial court pursued a policy of the patronage of higher learning, which could get him access to the centre, if he could convince the Chinese learned élite that he had something to interest them. He managed to get admission to the imperial court in Beijing in 1601. What he had to offer particularly, was astronomical and topographic scientific knowledge: he initially drew attention to himself by identifying the exact nature and purpose of astronomical instruments that had been set up by earlier scientists in the Chinese imperial court, whose use had in later periods been forgotten. He later constructed a world map in Chinese.

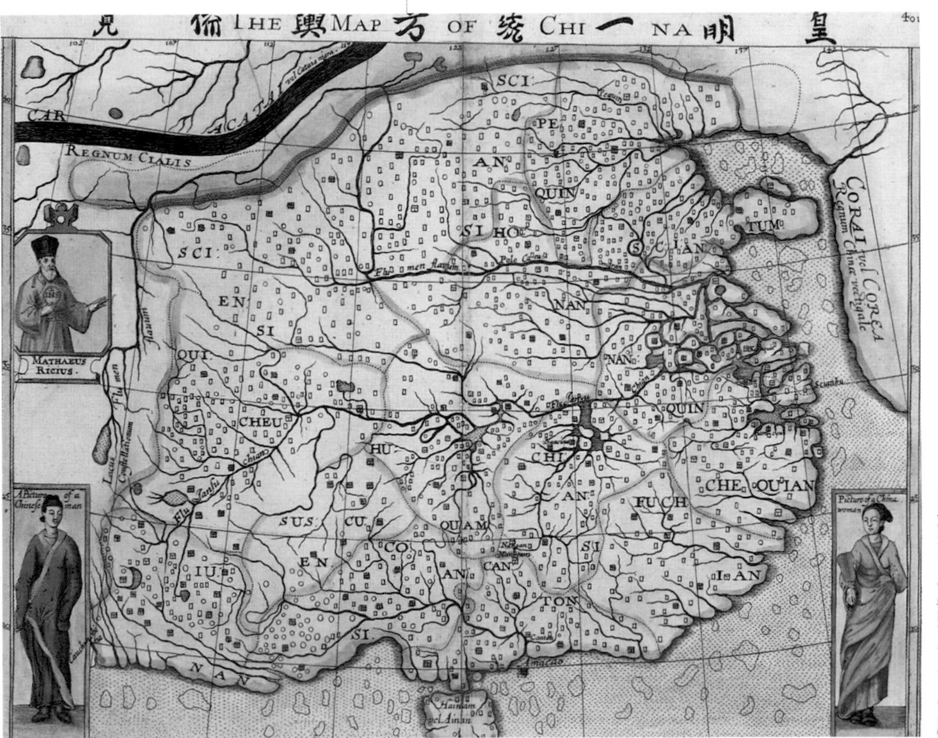

Ricci remained in the court until his death. He managed to convince some of the powerful figures there that Western Christian culture was not devoid of interest, and that its morality was in many respects reconcilable with Confucianism, although the main features of the Christian religion remained unintelligible to Chinese intellectuals. At the end of the century,

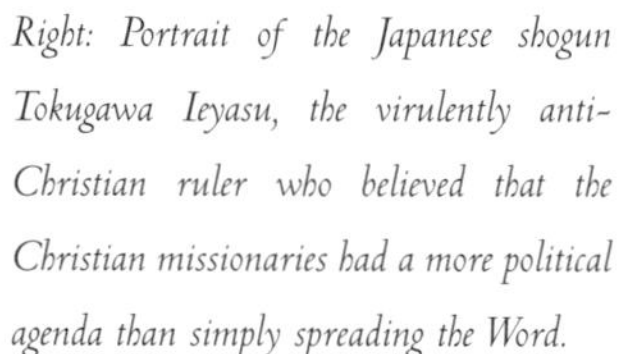

Right: Portrait of the Japanese shogun Tokugawa Ieyasu, the virulently anti-Christian ruler who believed that the Christian missionaries had a more political agenda than simply spreading the Word.

a time when Christian scholars were still present at court, a Chinese scholar made these concessions, but qualified them by saying: 'It is simply a shame that they speak of a Lord of Heaven, a crude and obnoxious conception that leads them into absurdities and which our literati have a great deal of difficulty in accepting.'[3]

The key to Ricci's dealings with Chinese culture was his policy of 'accommodation', which allowed Chinese converts to Christianity to retain certain features (although only certain ones) of Confucian practice, including ancestor worship, in their lives. He also accepted some Chinese religious terminology in his ritual practice conducted in the Chinese language, notably the terms for God; later missionaries changed Ricci's practice, but still drew on traditional Chinese religious terminology. There were some parallels in early Christianity for this, though it had to be admitted that in Christianity the debate had mostly swung in an exclusive and not an inclusive direction – one thinks of St Augustine's objections to pagan-style funeral meals round the tombs of ancestors.

These 'Chinese rites' were much criticized in Catholic Europe, and eventually, in the early eighteenth century, condemned by the popes. But the real missionary problems in China were perhaps not these. A capital difficulty was that Christianity had entered China through the imperial court and remained present in that court. The way in which Chinese bureaucracy dealt with Christian matters was always as a departmental responsibility of the imperial household, which much narrowed their national importance.

Missionary activity outside the imperial court was quite widespread, but always extremely precarious, and dependent on the favour of particular local and central officials. Missionaries constantly had to move on, and to leave their flocks for years without a pastor. A Chinese clergy was ordained, although only once in this period was there a Chinese bishop. Eventually, at the end of the eighteenth century and after the abolition of the Jesuit Order by the popes, the already very sporadic toleration of Christianity ceased, and the religion survived only in a clandestine way – less clandestine than in Japan, but still only existing for small and very isolated groups, which could only be reached by missionaries who operated secretly.

The Philippines were fully colonialized and fully Christianized. There was some established Christianity in Vietnam, and Christian southern India continued to exist round its very ancient base in Malabar, and in the Portuguese colony of Goa. Elsewhere in Asia, Christianity in the period before the great colonial thrusts of the nineteenth century remained, though widely spread, very much a modest minority movement.

By 1700 the guns and sails of the Europeans had taken Christianity all over the globe, from China to Peru. But whether it was a religion of the conquerors, or also the religion of the conquered, was not at all determined. Where Europeans were not, or not yet conquerors, its status was uncertain, as it still is in China. In the Islamic lands it was still a tolerated minority religion, as it had been from the beginning. However, the Eastern Christian churches almost without exception lived as a subordinate minority, where some centuries earlier they had possessed some independent political base. Only in the Russian lands did East Rome still thrive.

Above: An orthodox Christian icon from c. 1700, of St Nicholas of Mozhaisk.

1 A. Prosperi, 'New Heaven and New Earth', in *Prophetic Rome in the High Renaissance Period* (ed. M. Reeves, Oxford, 1992).

2 David D. Hall, *The Faithful Shepherd: A History of the New England Ministry in the Seventeenth Century* (Chapel Hill, 1972).

3 Quoted by R. G. Tiedemann, in *A World History of Christianity*, ed. A. Hastings (London, 1999), p.381.

7

The Rights of Man

Christendom had, since coming into existence, accepted the spiritual leadership of the men who prayed, even if Christians followed the warriors in battle, and obeyed the warrior caste as landowners. On the whole the initiative had stayed with the men of God during the period of the Church reforms in the sixteenth and seventeenth centuries, with the difference that the Protestant pastors placed the preaching of God's word above the offer of His sacraments. But at some point in the seventeenth or eighteenth centuries, a point that until the French Revolution of 1789 is hard to identify with any precision, the social initiative began to slip out of the hands of the churches. Christendom began to travel a long, on occasion painful road, through country in which God's ministers have seemed destined to become patients rather than central actors in the social process.

For centuries the sacred realm had in some sense included all the people of God, all the denizens of Christendom. Not a small company of the elect, but all humans in Christian society had for more than a millennium been thought of as in some way resident aliens on earth, whose real citizenship was in the city of God. St Augustine's vision had not gone unchallenged, even in the Middle Ages. But in the early modern period a transmutation of the role of the churches began, which arose not only as a result of the agitation of intellectuals and publicists, but also in the sense of a shift in the mysterious subsoil that underlies all social relationships.

Above: A seventeenth-century engraving of Hugh Peter (1598–1660), a Puritan clergyman and fiery preacher, who was also actively involved in parliamentary politics. Puritan political meddling could be treated by polemicists as the work of the devil.

Left: The Patriot Oath at the Anniversary of the Federation.

It was an extremely slow and for a long time hardly perceptible drift. Throughout Catholic Europe people continued to make Catholic deaths more or less in the way they had always done, continued to provide pious legacies, endow chapels, make penitential bequests, in ways that differed only slightly, if sometimes significantly, from the older practices. The villages, because of Tridentine reorganization and the provision of more seminaries, were subjected to more episcopal intervention, were more attentively directed, were subject to a closer penitential regime, in a sense more completely Christianized, than before. In certain country areas, it is true, there was not so much change. Even in country villages fifty or so miles from Rome, in the pope's own dominions, there were residual pagan practices and almost total religious ignorance, well into the nineteenth century.

But the fabric and decoration of the Catholic churches themselves were more closely supervised, in a manner that that was in many respects puritanical, even if certain approved images were reverenced and treasured. In the Protestant parishes there was compulsory church attendance, and pastoral supervision of the morals of the villagers. In Catholicism the great pilgrimages flourished, the Roman jubilees, the great gatherings of pilgrims in quest of special indulgences that been summoned to attend the Roman shrines at intervals of twenty-five years ever since the late Middle Ages, were well attended, and new devotions were introduced to the pious. Everywhere there was better census-taking and, on the whole, a better-disciplined Church. It did not in the least look like a gradual collapse of faith. But the social movement that enabled the brusque changes of the French Revolution to happen at ground level must in some way have been there.

The presupposition of the ancient parochial and monastic systems was the existence of lands and funds that had from much earlier times been given to the Church, that had in some sense been given to God. Such lands could still in Catholic countries amount to between a twelfth and a quarter of agricultural land, in Protestant countries much less; in the latter the pastor sometimes depended on a contract of maintenance granted by his congregation. In Catholic or in conservative Protestant countries such as England, the fact that the lands had been given to God did not stop the possessing families – or the state itself – from retaining substantial interests in them, either of a direct sort, or as a source of rights that gave employment to them or their nominees.

Beneath the ancient society other forces were at work. The state was gradually increasing its powers of intervention, so that the very ancient system – already abolished in some Protestant countries, but not in England – of treating a Church benefice as the object of private rights and not of public duties, was threatened. For example, the appearance of state educational systems was to threaten an ancient clerical monopoly in a far more fundamental way than the competition of secular private schools could have done. The birth of secular education had to wait upon the arrival of the French Revolution, but its spies were there before 1789 in some countries.

Christianity at the Court of Public Opinion

The so-called 'wars of religion' that had begun in the Reformation period, in which religion had played an increasingly minor role, ended in the 1648 Treaty of Westphalia that brought the Thirty Years War to a close in Germany. But the wars of religious opinion had yet to begin, in the sense of public controversy, not over the correct or incorrect doctrine of this Church or that, but over the principles upon which we should conduct discussion about religion, and the ways in which we should try to examine religious belief.

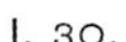
I. 30.

ENGLISH.

THE REVOLUTION.

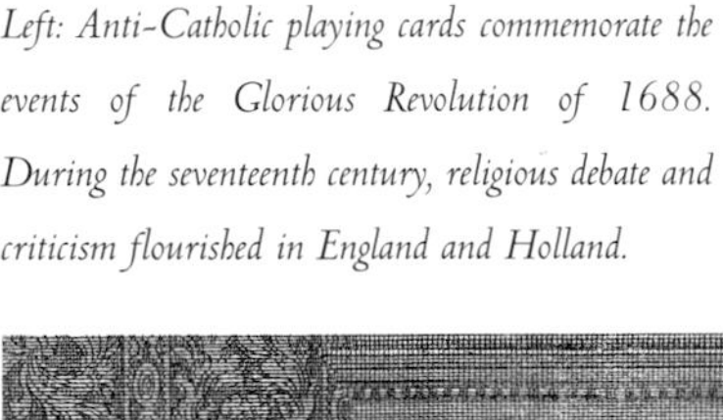
Left: Anti-Catholic playing cards commemorate the events of the Glorious Revolution of 1688. During the seventeenth century, religious debate and criticism flourished in England and Holland.

Above: A Dutch eighteenth-century engraving shows the signing of the Treaty of Utrecht, which ended the wars of Louis XIV.

Above: The Dutch philosopher Benedict Spinoza (1634–77). His Tractatus *published in 1670 was a devastating critique of the scriptures and a radical plea for philosophical freedom. It aroused enormous controversy and was banned in 1674.*

Such things were only possible in societies that were prepared to practise at least a selective religious toleration. Holland was intellectually the most tolerant society in Europe, and the great centre of publishing, not only of books, but also of that vehicle of early modern exchange of news and ideas, the periodical or gazette. Post-Restoration England, and even more the England that followed the Glorious Revolution of 1688, with its Anglo-Dutch leadership, was another place where religious debate was freer than elsewhere. But in the succeeding century, when the great wars of Louis XIV were over and more or less settled by the 1714 Treaty of Utrecht, the French nation that formerly had opposed a conformist Catholic front to Dutch Protestantism and secularism became the nation which, more than any other in Europe, nourished (as many believers thought) the rabid tribe of free-thinkers and libertines whose aim was to put Christianity on trial rather than to reform it.

The most radical of the early modern attempts to make a clean sweep of religious opinion, and thence a new start, was one of the earliest. Benedict (Baruch) Spinoza (1634–77) was a Dutch Jew of Iberian extraction whose change of name to Benedict had not indicated his conversion to Christianity, but perhaps pointed to his wish to show how equally things stood with him as to either religion. The *Theological-Political Treatise* that he published in Latin (*Tractatus Theologico-Politicus*) in 1670 contained a devastatingly critical examination of both Jewish and Christian scriptures, which by its exposure of their internal contradictions seemed (and still seems to the distinguished modern literary critic, George Steiner), to have left very little room for orthodox doctrine to survive in either religion. The tractate was also an attempt to establish from first principles a political philosophy of freedom, the noblest and most profound plea for freedom of opinion since the English poet Milton's *Areopagitica: A Speech for the Liberty of Unlicensed Printing* (1644). In it he wrote:

'...the object of government is not to change men from rational beings into beasts or puppets, but to enable them to develop their minds and bodies in security, and to employ their reason unshackled...In fact the true aim of government is liberty.'

Spinoza was understood in his own time as an ideological wrecker, whose only aim was to destroy the foundations of religion. The powerful ethical philosophy that he expounded, especially in his posthumously published *Ethica* (1677), was disregarded, although in moral theory also he set the agenda for the eighteenth century by proposing happiness as one of the main aims of man. His determinism was based upon false premises, but he still anticipated the following century in setting out an ethics that maintained that moral questions are factual questions.

Happiness, to Spinoza, could come only from the tranquillity that goes with the understanding of truth, a truth that he understood metaphysically. Here, at least, Spinoza was more attuned to his own society, which understood (as ours does not) the Socratic testimony that a philosopher may make as much impression by his life as by his arguments.[1] A century later the American Declaration of Rights was willing to take a much less moralistic and metaphysical view of the pursuit of happiness, which it classed as an 'inalienable right', along with life and liberty. But by then the pursuit of happiness had been linked with the practice of toleration. And the question 'Am I a just man?' had been replaced by the question 'Am I a happy man' ?

The philosophies of the eighteenth-century Enlightenment are rightly said to have been based on the new knowledge of the natural world that came from the understanding of science. It has to be added that the great Enlightenment publicists were not scientists, but above all popularizers of science. The trend was set by the French writer Bernard de Fontenelle (1657–1757), who, in 1686, published a *History of Oracles*, not very polite to miracles. Fontenelle set a polemic pattern for all later rationalist publicists by the critical examination of particular cases of supposed supernatural occurrences, such as the case of the gold tooth, in which a Silesian child had, in 1599, been reported to have had a molar tooth miraculously turned to gold. It was a sort of alleged miracle which still turns up in religious life today. Fontenelle later turned to the popularization of astronomy, in an essay in which he gallantly and with great wit and clarity explained the movements of the heavenly bodies to an imagined marquise.

The aim of the new philosophy was not to abolish religion, but to tame it. The prevailing tendency, from the English Shaftesbury (Third Earl, 1671–1713) to the French Voltaire (François Marie Arouet, 1694–1778) was deist, not atheist. Voltaire spoke for so many of his generation, when he wrote that his wish was to love God, whom he sought as a father; but the God actually shown for his worship was someone he could only describe as a hateful tyrant, who offered man nothing but an insoluble enigma. The problem, of which he did not despair of an answer, was to humanize God: human nature was to be vindicated.

The English were especially fertile in ways of thought that would preserve a religion reconcilable with science, which was compatible with the principles of rational natural philosophy. In 1730 Matthew Tindal (1656–1733) published *Christianity as old as the Creation, or the Gospel – a Republication of the Law of Nature.* It was in order to preserve a rational natural theology that George Berkeley, Bishop of Cloyne (1685–1753), composed his very powerful and influential *Principles of Human Knowledge* (1710). His intention was to defend natural theology against the mechanistic tendencies that he detected in the English philosopher John Locke's *Essay Concerning Human Understanding* (1690), which Berkeley rightly interpreted as a work that would become a great support for sceptical views about religion.

Behind the endless reasonings of Voltaire lay the mathematically viewed universe of Isaac Newton (1643–1727), of whose scientific thought Voltaire was the tireless popularizer. On this basis Voltaire conceived a universe of which God was the benevolent, omnipresent sovereign, whose providence is presumed to reward good and to punish evil, and who comes to the aid of the poor and oppressed, but whose actions are entirely impenetrable to man. That Newton had in fact spent his declining years practising alchemy and speculating on biblical chronology as it could be strictly and literally understood from scripture, worried neither Voltaire nor his readers. Voltaire's universe assumed optimism, but he himself felt that optimism was impossible: that was the message of his great novel, *Candide* (1759), the doubting man's edition of the Book of Job.

Unlike Voltaire, both Denis Diderot (1713–84) and Jean d'Alembert (1717–83) were atheistic rather than than deist. In Diderot, especially, the transition between the reasonable man and the man of sentiment took place, which was to bring the new intellectuals towards the assertion of individual consciousness and of Romantic experience. With Jean-Jaques Rousseau (1712–78) this assertion was

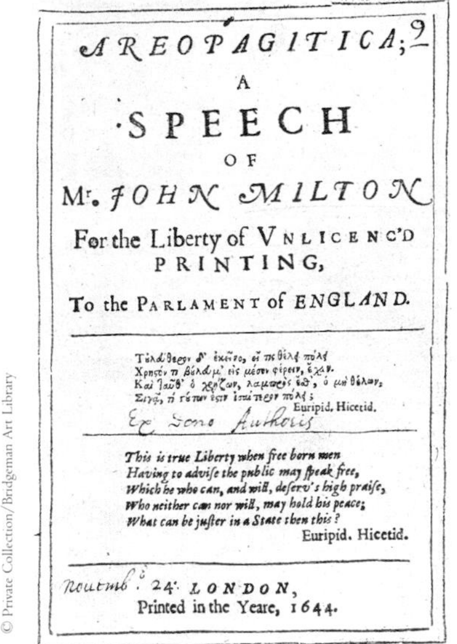
AREOPAGITICA;
A
SPEECH
OF
Mr. JOHN MILTON
For the Liberty of VNLICENC'D
PRINTING,
To the PARLAMENT of ENGLAND.

Euripid. Hicetid.

This is true Liberty when free born men
Having to advise the public may speak free,
Which he who can, and will, deserv's high praise,
Who neither can nor will, may hold his peace;
What can be juster in a State then this?
Euripid. Hicetid.

LONDON,
Printed in the Yeare, 1644.

Above: The frontispiece of John Milton's Areopagitica. *Published in 1644, it remains a rallying cry for freedom of the press.*

Below: Portrait of François Marie Arouet de Voltaire, one of the great figures of the eighteenth-century Enlightenment. He attacked religious bigotry but not God, whom he sought to humanize.

Above: A telescope belonging to Sir Isaac Newton. Newton's scientific view of the universe profoundly influenced Enlightenment thought.

Below: an engraving of an instrument-maker's workshop and tools from Diderot's Encyclopédie.

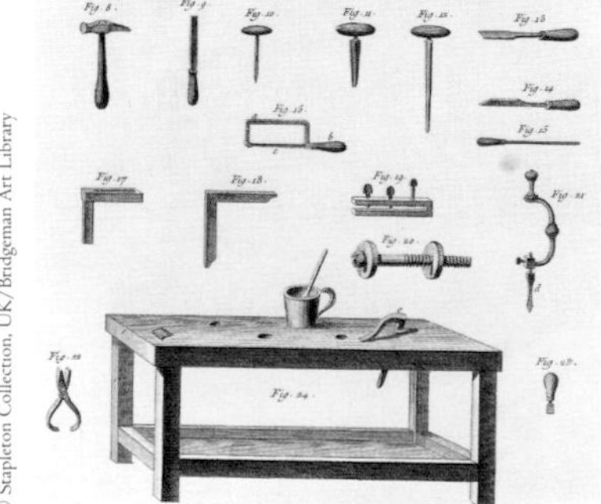

brought into the mainstream of European literary consciousness. Although Rousseau sustained that the integrity of a 'pure' religion was possible, his morality of sentiment was irreconcilable with traditional Christian doctrine:

'I have seen that, in order to act well with pleasure, I have to act freely and without fear; if I want to lose the pleasant feeling of carrying out a good work, I have only to feel it a duty.' (Sixième Promenade)

The Enlightenment, as it started to call itself within in its own lifetime, was a huge operation of public information and publication, of which the *Encyclopédie* (1751–65) of Diderot was the extraordinary and crowning achievement. In the *Encyclopédie* there lay in germ all the techniques of popular, rationalist publicity, as they were to survive in the Society for the Diffusion of Useful Knowledge (founded by the Utilitarians in 1827), in the public libraries and reading rooms of the nineteenth century, in the BBC Brains Trusts of the 1940s and 1950s, and in the CD and Internet information facilities of our own times.

Revolution in the New World

The American Revolution against British colonial government that occurred in 1776 was important to the churches both inside and outside North America. The revolution of the colonists was the first great political success of the European Enlightenment; it made the little successes of the Encyclopédistes, the currying of the favour of the 'enlightened' Frederick the Great of Prussia by Voltaire, or that of Catherine the Great by Diderot, look very petty. Those who made the American Revolution were almost to a man 'enlightened' in a general sense, and Freemasonry, the new convivial and fraternal organization that was at that time the badge of enlightened rationalism, was common among their leaders. Not for nothing was the Freemason sign of the eye and the pyramid placed on the Great Seal of the United States, and on the obverse of the one dollar bills. The English ex-Quaker Thomas Paine (1737–1809) happened to find himself in Philadelphia in 1776: his pamphlet *Common Sense*, which called clearly for independence, was one of the most important documents of the immediate prehistory of the American Revolution. To it he added a postscript that reproached the Quakers for their disavowing resistance to the English crown. Thomas Paine was among several Americans (for he became an American) who linked the American with the French Revolution, in his case by his second famous pamphlet, *The Rights of Man* (1791–2).

The American Revolution was very different from its French successor in its relationship with the Churches. In France the Revolution was to slice civil society in two, and to produce a wounding break in Europe between enlightened principles and those of the Churches, which has in some respects still, after two centuries, not fully healed. In the Amercan colonies the Churches were on the whole behind the rebellion. Catholics fought on the American side in the Revolutionary War, and a Congregational minister, George Witherspoon, and a Catholic layman, Charles Carroll, were among the signatories to the Declaration of Independence.

Internally the American Revolution only strengthened the existing Church settlement in the ex-colonies. Article 6 of the Constitution (1787) excluded any religious test as a qualification for public office in the United States, and the First Amendment (1791) forbade Congress to make any law that either concerned the establishment of religion or restricted its free exercise. Free rights to exercise

IN CONGRESS, JULY 4, 1776.

The unanimous Declaration of the thirteen united States of America,

When in the Course of human events, it becomes necessary for one people to dissolve the political bands which have connected them with another, and to assume among the powers of the earth, the separate and equal station to which the Laws of Nature and of Nature's God entitle them, a decent respect to the opinions of mankind requires that they should declare the causes which impel them to the separation. — We hold these truths to be self-evident, that all men are created equal, that they are endowed by their Creator with certain unalienable Rights, that among these are Life, Liberty and the pursuit of Happiness. — That to secure these rights, Governments are instituted among Men, deriving their just powers from the consent of the governed, — That whenever any Form of Government becomes destructive of these ends, it is the Right of the People to alter or to abolish it, and to institute new Government, laying its foundation on such principles and organizing its powers in such form, as to them shall seem most likely to effect their Safety and Happiness. Prudence, indeed, will dictate that Governments long established should not be changed for light and transient causes; and accordingly all experience hath shewn, that mankind are more disposed to suffer, while evils are sufferable, than to right themselves by abolishing the forms to which they are accustomed. But when a long train of abuses and usurpations, pursuing invariably the same Object evinces a design to reduce them under absolute Despotism, it is their right, it is their duty, to throw off such Government, and to provide new Guards for their future security. — Such has been the patient sufferance of these Colonies; and such is now the necessity which constrains them to alter their former Systems of Government. The history of the present King of Great Britain is a history of repeated injuries and usurpations, all having in direct object the establishment of an absolute Tyranny over these States. To prove this, let Facts be submitted to a candid world. — He has refused his Assent to Laws, the most wholesome and necessary for the public good. — He has forbidden his Governors to pass Laws of immediate and pressing importance, unless suspended in their operation till his Assent should be obtained; and when so suspended, he has utterly neglected to attend to them. — He has refused to pass other Laws for the accommodation of large districts of people, unless those people would relinquish the right of Representation in the Legislature, a right inestimable to them and formidable to tyrants only. — He has called together legislative bodies at places unusual, uncomfortable, and distant from the depository of their Public Records, for the sole purpose of fatiguing them into compliance with his measures. — He has dissolved Representative Houses repeatedly, for opposing with manly firmness his invasions on the rights of the people. — He has refused for a long time, after such dissolutions, to cause others to be elected; whereby the Legislative powers, incapable of Annihilation, have returned to the People at large for their exercise; the State remaining in the mean time exposed to all the dangers of invasion from without, and convulsions within. — He has endeavoured to prevent the population of these States; for that purpose obstructing the Laws for Naturalization of Foreigners; refusing to pass others to encourage their migrations hither, and raising the conditions of new Appropriations of Lands. — He has obstructed the Administration of Justice, by refusing his Assent to Laws for establishing Judiciary powers. — He has made Judges dependent on his Will alone, for the tenure of their offices, and the amount and payment of their salaries. — He has erected a multitude of New Offices, and sent hither swarms of Officers to harrass our people, and eat out their substance. — He has kept among us, in times of peace, Standing Armies without the Consent of our legislatures. — He has affected to render the Military independent of and superior to the Civil power. — He has combined with others to subject us to a jurisdiction foreign to our constitution, and unacknowledged by our laws; giving his Assent to their Acts of pretended Legislation: — For Quartering large bodies of armed troops among us: — For protecting them, by a mock Trial, from punishment for any Murders which they should commit on the Inhabitants of these States: — For cutting off our Trade with all parts of the world: — For imposing Taxes on us without our Consent: — For depriving us in many cases, of the benefits of Trial by Jury: — For transporting us beyond Seas to be tried for pretended offences — For abolishing the free System of English Laws in a neighbouring Province, establishing therein an Arbitrary government, and enlarging its Boundaries so as to render it at once an example and fit instrument for introducing the same absolute rule into these Colonies: — For taking away our Charters, abolishing our most valuable Laws, and altering fundamentally the Forms of our Governments: — For suspending our own Legislatures, and declaring themselves invested with power to legislate for us in all cases whatsoever. — He has abdicated Government here, by declaring us out of his Protection and waging War against us. — He has plundered our seas, ravaged our Coasts, burnt our towns, and destroyed the lives of our people. — He is at this time transporting large Armies of foreign Mercenaries to compleat the works of death, desolation and tyranny, already begun with circumstances of Cruelty & perfidy scarcely paralleled in the most barbarous ages, and totally unworthy the Head of a civilized nation. — He has constrained our fellow Citizens taken Captive on the high Seas to bear Arms against their Country, to become the executioners of their friends and Brethren, or to fall themselves by their Hands. — He has excited domestic insurrections amongst us, and has endeavoured to bring on the inhabitants of our frontiers, the merciless Indian Savages, whose known rule of warfare, is an undistinguished destruction of all ages, sexes and conditions. In every stage of these Oppressions We have Petitioned for Redress in the most humble terms: Our repeated Petitions have been answered by repeated injury. A Prince, whose character is thus marked by every act which may define a Tyrant, is unfit to be the ruler of a free people. Nor have We been wanting in attentions to our Brittish brethren. We have warned them from time to time of attempts by their legislature to extend an unwarrantable jurisdiction over us. We have reminded them of the circumstances of our emigration and settlement here. We have appealed to their native justice and magnanimity, and we have conjured them by the ties of our common kindred to disavow these usurpations, which, would inevitably interrupt our connections and correspondence. They too have been deaf to the voice of justice and of consanguinity. We must, therefore, acquiesce in the necessity, which denounces our Separation, and hold them, as we hold the rest of mankind, Enemies in War, in Peace Friends. —

We, therefore, the Representatives of the united States of America, in General Congress, Assembled, appealing to the Supreme Judge of the world for the rectitude of our intentions, do, in the Name, and by Authority of the good People of these Colonies, solemnly publish and declare, That these United Colonies are, and of Right ought to be Free and Independent States; that they are Absolved from all Allegiance to the British Crown, and that all political connection between them and the State of Great Britain, is and ought to be totally dissolved; and that as Free and Independent States, they have full Power to levy War, conclude Peace, contract Alliances, establish Commerce, and to do all other Acts and Things which Independent States may of right do. — And for the support of this Declaration, with a firm reliance on the protection of divine Providence, we mutually pledge to each other our Lives, our Fortunes and our sacred Honor.

John Hancock

Button Gwinnett
Lyman Hall
Geo Walton.

Wm Hooper
Joseph Hewes,
John Penn

Edward Rutledge 1.

Thos Heyward Junr.
Thomas Lynch Junr.
Arthur Middleton

Samuel Chase
Wm. Paca
Thos. Stone
Charles Carroll of Carrollton

George Wythe
Richard Henry Lee
Th Jefferson
Benja Harrison
Thos Nelson jr.
Francis Lightfoot Lee
Carter Braxton

Robt Morris
Benjamin Rush
Benja. Franklin
John Morton
Geo Clymer
Jas. Smith
Geo. Taylor
James Wilson
Geo. Ross

Caesar Rodney
Geo Read
Tho M:Kean

Wm Floyd
Phil. Livingston
Frans. Lewis
Lewis Morris

Richd. Stockton
Jno Witherspoon
Fras. Hopkinson
John Hart
Abra Clark

Josiah Bartlett
Wm. Whipple
Saml Adams
John Adams
Robt Treat Paine
Elbridge Gerry
Step Hopkins
William Ellery
Roger Sherman
Saml Huntington
Wm Williams
Oliver Wolcott
Matthew Thornton

THE DECLARATION OF INDEPENDENCE

On July 4, 1776, the Continental Congress adopted the Declaration of Independence, whereby the United Colonies of America declared themselves to be "Free and Independent States." After the Declaration had been engrossed on parchment, it was signed on August 2 by the delegates to the Congress who were present and later by others. It is now on permanent display in the National Archives. A copper-plate engraving, produced by direct impression from the document itself, was completed by William J. Stone in 1823. The above reproduction is made from one of Stone's facsimiles.

Left: The Declaration of Independence issued on 4 July 1776 by the American colonies. Signatories to this revolutionary document included a Congregational minister and Catholic layman.

Above: 'Who Wants Me?' – a cartoon by the English caricaturist Isaac Cruikshank showing the American revolutionary Tom Paine and his pamphlet The Rights of Man, *which supported the French Revolution.*

religion were also written into the constitutions of the individual states. The New England states retained a degree of establishment of the Congregationalist churches on the English model, but in four of the thirteen colonies including Pennsylvania, there was no religious establishment of any sort. Establishment remained, however, a possible state option that was to be taken up by the Mormons in Utah in the nineteenth century.

Revolution in Europe

Churchmen were, almost as much as any other social group in the eighteenth century, penetrated by the principles of the Enlightenment. In spite of papal prohibition, the number of Freemason priests in Catholic countries was considerable. The most notable demonstration of papal weakness came about because of a chain of circumstances arising from Jesuit reluctance to go along with a Spanish-Portuguese colonial decision of 1750. This would have compelled them to submit to a huge forced movement of populations from Jesuit-run Paraguay. The decision would have inflicted – and did inflict – appalling hardship on the Paraguay Indians, compelling them to move out of the area and across the River Uruguay.

From these beginnings arose a persecution of the Jesuits in Portugal, and a virtual coalition of their many European enemies in governments all over the continent, to put pressure on Rome to their disfavour. A financial scandal in France made their situation yet worse, so far as general European opinion went. Although Pope Clement XIII refused to abandon them, his successor, Pope Clement XIV (pope 1769–74) was made of weaker stuff. In 1773 he signed the bull of suppression of the whole Jesuit Order, which the Order, bound by its own constitution to obedience to the pope, had to obey. It was a great triumph of Enlightenment political correctness that earned Pope Clement XIV a condescending pat on the back in the memoirs of the English historian, Edward Gibbon. And in a sense it was a pointer towards the direction things were later to take in France, where the most radical consequences were to follow from reformist correctness among the privileged classes.

In the critical meetings of the French Estates General in the summer of 1789, a majority of the estate of the clergy joined the Third Estate after the oath of the tennis court. The decision was influenced by the discontents of the lower clergy, but turned out to be suicidal for their order. The financial consequences were swift; in November, 1789 Church property was nationalized, and the clergy became state employees. In such circumstances the monasteries could not survive. In 1790 the Civil Constitution of the Clergy formally nationalized the Church itself. Bishoprics became the ecclesiastical shadows of the new civil departments; bishops and priests were to be elected by the congregations; papal intervention was forbidden.

There had been precedents for some of these things in earlier French Gallicanism, which the French kings had promoted from the later Middle Ages into the early modern period as a doctrine that asserted the rights of the French Church to a certain limited independence from the papacy. In theory, Church doctrine was not affected by the Civil Constitution of 1790, but in effect it created a new Church that was unacceptable to many of its own clergy. Later in the year an oath of allegiance to the state and to the civil constitution of the clergy was required, forcing many of the clergy into emigration or schism. More than half the clergy refused the oath, and in 1791 the pope condemned the civil constitution as sacrilegious. In the Terror of 1792, hundreds of the clergy were murdered or

Above: Thomas Jefferson's design for the Great Seal of the United States of America. The pyramid sign of the Freemasons, symbol of enlightened rationalism, shines out between Liberty and Justice, who support a coat of arms surrounded by the initials of the thirteen colonies.

Below: Great Salt Lake, Utah, where, in the nineteenth century, the Mormons took the state option to set up a religious community.

© Palazzo Barberini/Bridgeman Art Library

Left: A Jesuit and his family by Marco Benefiale (1684–1764). Clement XIV suppressed the Jesuit Order in 1773.

Below: The Tennis Court Oath taken on 20 June 1789 by delegates of the Third Estate, who swore not to disband until France had a constitution.

© Musée Carnavalet, Paris, France/Bridgeman Art Library

executed, and a vast emigration, in all some 30,000, took place: the Convention continued to execute priests into 1793, and there was a second outburst of persecution at the end of the decade.

The Declaration of the Rights of Man in 1789 was integrally connected with the abolition of privilege that lay behind the huge seizures of Church property, but not the claim to complete control of the Church – that had a much more complex prehistory. In general the ideological novelty of the Revolution lay much more in its assertion of national right. This was very shortly to give rise in the Revolutionary and Napoleonic Wars to the fearsome series of modern European national wars which, until recent events in the Balkans, was thought to be over.

The settlement of the Revolutionary crisis of the French Church took place, not because of an internal movement, but as the result of external military conquests. In 1796 Napoleon's armies marched into central Italy. Military resistance collapsed, and French puppet republics were set up. Early in the following year he occupied the papal states, and plundered the remaining treasures of the great shrine to the Mother of Christ at Loreto, near the Adriatic coast. Not far from Loreto, in the little hill town of Tolentino, he imposed an onerous treaty upon Pope Pius VI (pope 1775–99), which included the concession to plunder works of art in the papal dominions. Subsequently the death of a French general in an anti-French riot in Rome led to the end of even relative independence for the pope as a secular ruler. The rest of the papal states were occupied, and a puppet Roman republic established, preparatory to the French invasion of southern Italy. Only Sicily remained Roman Catholic and non-French, defended by the Protestant fleet of Nelson.

Below: A cartoon showing Church and nobility recoiling in fear from the Third Estate. By August 1789, clergy and nobles had been forced to relinquish their privileges.

© Giraudon/Bridgeman Art Library

Above: Political cartoon showing Napoleon Bonaparte as King of Rome. In 1796, during the Revolutionary Wars, Napoleon marched into Italy and in early 1797 occupied the papal states.

Right: The Declaration of the Rights of Man and Citizen, adopted by the Constituent Assembly in France in 1789. Like the American Declaration of Independence, it carries the sign of the Freemasons.

Below: The Madonna of Loretto *by the Italian artist Raphael. By a treaty signed with the pope in 1797, the conquering Napoleon could take what fine art he wished from the papal territories.*

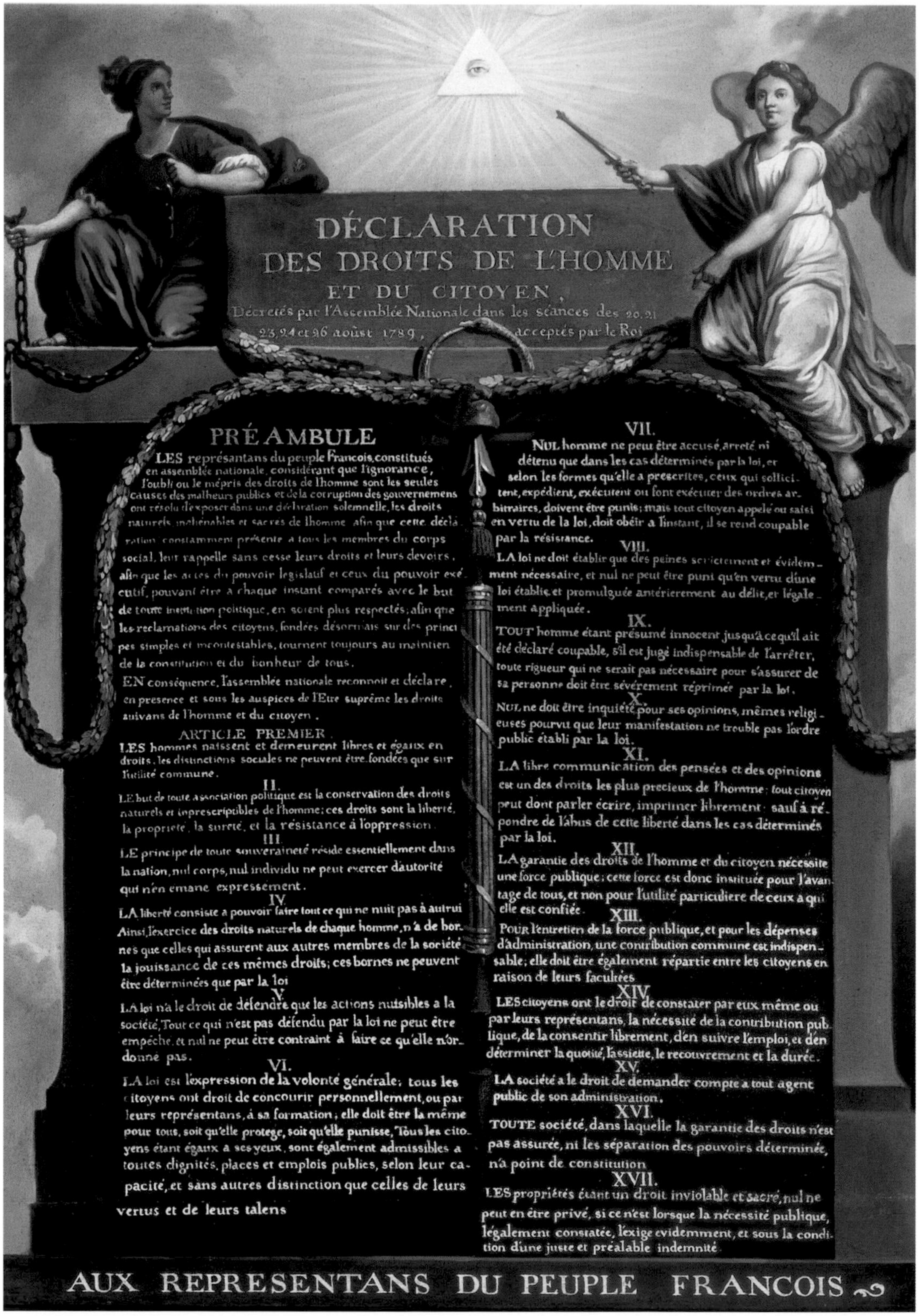

DÉCLARATION DES DROITS DE L'HOMME ET DU CITOYEN,

Décrétés par l'Assemblée Nationale dans les séances des 20, 21, 23, 24 et 26 aoûst 1789, acceptés par le Roi

PRÉAMBULE

LES représantans du peuple Francois, constitués en assemblée nationale, considérant que l'ignorance, l'oubli ou le mépris des droits de l'homme sont les seules causes des malheurs publics et de la corruption des gouvernemens ont résolu d'exposer dans une déclaration solemnelle, les droits naturels, inaliénables et sacrés de l'homme afin que cette déclaration constamment présente à tous les membres du corps social, leur rappelle sans cesse leurs droits et leurs devoirs, afin que les actes du pouvoir legislatif et ceux du pouvoir exécutif, pouvant être à chaque instant comparés avec le but de toute institution politique, en soient plus respectés; afin que les reclamations des citoyens, fondées désormais sur des principes simples et incontestables, tournent toujours au maintien de la constitution et du bonheur de tous.

EN conséquence, l'assemblée nationale reconnoit et déclare, en presence et sous les auspices de l'Etre suprême les droits suivans de l'homme et du citoyen.

ARTICLE PREMIER.

LES hommes naissent et demeurent libres et égaux en droits. les distinctions sociales ne peuvent être fondées que sur l'utilité commune.

II.

LE but de toute association politique est la conservation des droits naturels et inprescriptibles de l'homme: ces droits sont la liberté, la propriété, la sureté, et la résistance à l'oppression.

III.

LE principe de toute souveraineté réside essentiellement dans la nation, nul corps, nul individu ne peut exercer d'autorité qui n'en emane expressément.

IV.

LA liberté consiste a pouvoir faire tout ce qui ne nuit pas à autrui Ainsi, l'exercice des droits naturels de chaque homme, n'a de bornes que celles qui assurent aux autres membres de la société la jouissance de ces mêmes droits; ces bornes ne peuvent être déterminées que par la loi

V.

LA loi n'a le droit de défendre que les actions nuisibles a la société, Tout ce qui n'est pas défendu par la loi ne peut être empêché, et nul ne peut être contraint à faire ce qu'elle n'ordonne pas.

VI.

LA loi est l'expression de la volonté générale; tous les citoyens ont droit de concourir personnellement, ou par leurs représentans, à sa formation; elle doit être la même pour tous, soit qu'elle protege, soit qu'elle punisse, Tous les citoyens étant égaux a ses yeux, sont également admissibles a toutes dignités, places et emplois publics, selon leur capacité, et sans autres distinction que celles de leurs vertus et de leurs talens

VII.

NUL homme ne peut être accusé, arreté ni détenu que dans les cas déterminés par la loi, et selon les formes qu'elle a prescrites, ceux qui sollicitent, expédient, exécutent ou font exécuter des ordres arbitraires, doivent être punis; mais tout citoyen appelé ou saisi en vertu de la loi, doit obéir a l'instant, il se rend coupable par la résistance.

VIII.

LA loi ne doit établir que des peines strictement et évidemment nécessaire, et nul ne peut être puni qu'en vertu d'une loi établie et promulguée antérierement au délit, et légalement appliquée.

IX.

TOUT homme étant présumé innocent jusqu'à ce qu'il ait été déclaré coupable, s'il est jugé indispensable de l'arrêter, toute rigueur qui ne serait pas nécessaire pour s'assurer de sa personne doit être sévérement réprimée par la loi.

X.

NUL ne doit être inquiété pour ses opinions, mêmes religieuses pourvu que leur manifestation ne trouble pas l'ordre public établi par la loi.

XI.

LA libre communication des pensées et des opinions est un des droits les plus precieux de l'homme; tout citoyen peut dont parler écrire, imprimer librement: sauf à répondre de l'abus de cette liberté dans les cas déterminés par la loi.

XII.

LA garantie des droits de l'homme et du citoyen nécessite une force publique: cette force est donc instituée pour l'avantage de tous, et non pour l'utilité particuliere de ceux a qui elle est confiée.

XIII.

POUR l'entretien de la force publique, et pour les dépenses d'administration, une contribution commune est indispensable; elle doit être également répartie entre les citoyens en raison de leurs facultées

XIV.

LES citoyens ont le droit de constater par eux même ou par leurs représentans, la nécessité de la contribution publique, de la consentir librement, d'en suivre l'emploi, et d'en déterminer la quotité, l'assiette, le recouvrement et la durée.

XV.

LA société a le droit de demander compte a tout agent public de son administration.

XVI.

TOUTE société, dans laquelle la garantie des droits n'est pas assurée, ni les séparation des pouvoirs déterminée, n'a point de constitution

XVII.

LES propriétés étant un droit inviolable et sacré, nul ne peut en être privé, si ce n'est lorsque la nécessité publique, légalement constatée, l'exige evidemment, et sous la condition d'une juste et préalable indemnité.

AUX REPRESENTANS DU PEUPLE FRANCOIS

After a stay in Tuscany, Pope Pius VI, who was an old and dying man, was carried under guard over the Alpine passes in the spring of 1799 to Grenoble in France, to be taken as a prisoner to Valence on the Rhone, where he died that summer. In southern Italy ferocious peasant counter-revolutionary wars of rebellion were waged against the French, supported by English sea power: other similar Catholic peasant wars were fought in Belgium, Switzerland, and in the west of France itself.

Pope Pius VI's successor, Pius VII (pope 1800–21) was elected in Austrian Venice. In 1801 he agreed a concordat with Napoleon that regulated the situation of the Church in France for a over a century. The new French Church was to be in some respects (but only some) the Gallican Church desired by the old French monarchy, but in others a quite different, modernized affair. Catholicism was recognized as the majority religion in France, though not as the state religion: the bishops and clergy (now salaried state employees) were to swear an oath of allegiance to the state. The pope in effect acquired new powers, not available to his predecessors, over French bishops, whom he was enabled to dismiss or confirm. The confiscation of Church property was accepted. It is significant that, after the fall and defeat of Napoleon, the restored French royalist government after 1815 was unable to find a preferable solution, and left the Napoleonic concordat intact. Napoleon and Pope Pius VII had found an agreement that was to influence all modern government thinking in Catholic countries.

Pope Pius VII's later functions at the coronation of Napoleon as French emperor in 1804 at Notre Dame in Paris were really only a postscript to the concordat. In 1806 an event of far more significance took place in Vienna: the resignation by the Austrian ruler Francis II of the title of Holy Roman Emperor. The Christendom that had come into existence after Charlemagne's coronation in 800 had come to an end, even though many of the mentalities of Christendom still persisted.

Evangelical Revival and Awakening in Protestantism

After these events in the great public world of war and revolution, the affairs of modest pastors in England and North America may seem small beer. But the evangelical revivals in Protestant lands are not to be disregarded, because they were to help decide a new social context for modern Christianity.

There is no older theme in Christianity than the awakening of the troubled soul, and the desire of the awakened soul to abide with kindred spirits who may give it some comfort. In the traditions of both Lutheranism and Calvinism there was much to this purpose that was by no means crowded out by the onset of early rationalism.

But the conversion – as it later came to be called – of the troubled soul can be a socially disturbing process. In the eighteenth century, Anglicanism was a Church that was closely tied to the defence of a particular theory of constitutional government and a particular dynasty, that of the Hanoverians. It possessed many learned and moderate bishops, who on the whole saw

Below: Napoleon at his coronation as emperor in 1804 (painted by Ingres). Pope Pius VII presided, a logical consequence of the 1801 concordat that re-established the Roman Catholic Church in France.

Below: John Wesley, charismatic preacher and founder of Methodism, visiting his mother's grave.

enthusiasm in religion as a threat to established and reasonable order. Hanoverian Anglicanism may from the distance of a couple of centuries seem a quiet place where clergymen ate their dinners undisturbed, but the memory of a disputed royal succession in which religion was a central issue, and even the present threat of Jacobite revolution, were very much alive. To the eighteenth-century ruling classes, for whom the clergy formed, either as preachers or as magistrates, a sort of highly privileged police force, fear of the mob was a potent thing, even when it marched to anti-papist slogans.

The onset of religious enthusiasm in the Church of England was quite a complex affair, which was bound up on one side of the Atlantic with the German connections of the Hanoverian monarchy, and on the other with the common religious world still inhabited by the Protestantism of the British homeland, and that of the North American colonists. The English religious revivalism, which could never be called religious revolution, started in a quite low-key way among young clergymen who were of modest origins, but had attended Oxford or Cambridge colleges – in fact the key figure, John Wesley (1703–91), the son of an engaging but badly organized Anglican clergyman, looked set to make a very orthodox clerical career, founded on his fellowship of Lincoln College.

The careers of John Wesley and his brother Charles, and that of their Oxford contemporary, also to become a clergyman, George Whitefield (1714–70), were for some time intertwined. John Wesley and Whitefield were both to become compelling preachers, but there was something more dramatic about Whitefield, which caused congregations practically to mob him. Wesley, on the other hand, seems to have stimulated demonstrations that would now be called charismatic. The foundation of his ministry was what his own father called 'the inward witness', an assurance of election for salvation. Of the two, Wesley was the more resistant to Calvinist formulation of doctrine, but far from doctrinally consistent.

What principally influenced Wesley in the earlier stages of his ministry was the Moravian Brethren, a sect with a long history in northern Germany, which experienced a great revival in the early eighteenth century that took them both to England and to the North American colonies. It might be said to have been part of a long on-and-off love affair between English and German intellectuals. The British intellectuals tended to be beguiled both by German devotion to intellectual 'system', which was a key word in much Enlightenment discourse, and by the powerful emotional charge that informed so much of Germanic philosophical and religious speculation.

Both John Wesley and Whitefield, at early stages of their careers, went as missionaries for a time to Georgia in the south of the American colonies. For Wesley the experience was important but not decisive; for Whitefield, whose experiences in New England were more positive, it may have been more important. But the decisive episodes in the ministries of both Whitefield and Wesley sprang out of Whitefield's open-air preaching campaigns in the mining areas outside Bristol, in 1739.

These huge outdoor gatherings – which would not have seemed strange to St Francis – inspired Wesley and his followers to preach particularly in the industrializing mining zones of the Midlands, which would seem to modern people still like open countryside, but were especially fertile for the mission field because the established parochial system did not cater for them. Both within and out of doors, the hymns that John Wesley and his brother Charles composed were to become an integral part of collective worship. The tradition and the organization for which Wesley was responsible, meant the foundation of a body that had the flexibility to respond swiftly to the enormous demands that industrialization was going to make on the Christian apostolate, especially when, as so often happened, the new mines and factories were in areas where the existing parochial system was unable to cope with them. The members of Wesley's 'Societies' were called 'Methodists', an appellation which they owed in part to their centralized organization, based on the principle of 'connexion'. Their direct and indirect influence on English religious and social life was to be enormous, especially as it was to be transmitted in partly secularized form into the twentieth century because of Methodist influence on trade unions and the nascent Labour Party.

Below: George Whitefield, a leading figure in the English religious revivalism of the eighteenth century, preaching to a rapt audience in the countryside.

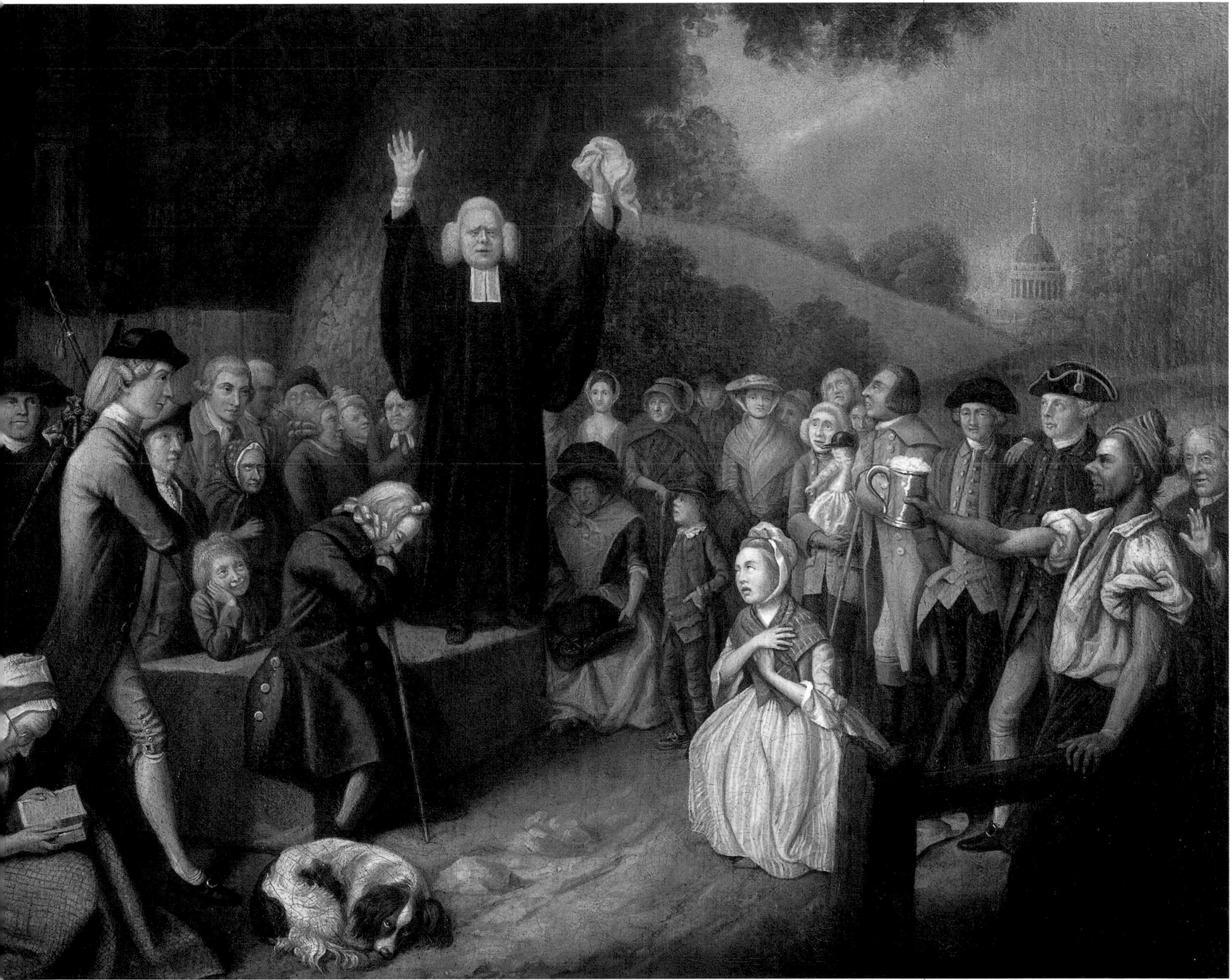

© Private Collection/Bridgeman Art Library

Right: The first Methodist Episcopal Church in North America. From its founding, Methodism spread rapidly, causing a clash with the Anglicans. Wesley ordained Thomas Coke (1747–1818) to superintend the 'brethren in America'.

Wesley refused to accept any limits on his preaching mission. He wrote that:

'...I look upon all the world as my parish: thus far, I mean, that in whatever part of it I am, I judge it meet, right and my bounden duty to declare unto all that are willing to hear the glad tidings of salvation.'

Wesley and his preachers were not always popular. Especially in the earlier stages, they gave cause to rioting and violence, and they were not only reviled but persecuted, and in one or two cases virtually martyred. The established order was not at all disposed to protect them, and occasionally left them under mob attack.

Wesley was to the end of his long life unwilling to admit that he had founded a dissenting sect. He declared his utter unwillingness to leave the Church of England, only a couple of years before his death. On the other hand, Methodism, as his way of doing things was called, required organization that the Anglican Church could not and would not provide. He could run the exhausting business of covering huge areas of the country with preaching 'circuits', only with the help of lay preachers whom he appointed, preachers who were to lead exacting lives of poverty and service. He also, towards the end of his life, had ordained men for the ministry in America and Scotland, some as 'superintendents'. This was not really reconcilable with continued Anglicanism.

Both in England and in North America, the eighteenth century proved to be a time in which, despite the surrounding rationalism, the Protestant churches and sects could find men and women who were profoundly convinced about religious truth, and willing to devote their lives to teaching and preaching, often in the uncongenial surroundings of the new industries. To some extent, this period of the 'Great Awakenings' made itself felt upon the black slave communities of America, but the impact was very limited.

The question of slavery and of black subjection remained. Among the sects, only the Quakers, late in the eighteenth century, denied membership to slave owners, as a result of the efforts of the Quaker tailor, John Woolman (1720–72). An American evangelical divine, Samuel Hopkins, published in 1776, at the start of the Independence war, *A Dialogue Concerning the Slavery of the Africans,* which pointed out that 'the sons of liberty' were 'oppressing and tyrannizing over many thousands of poor blacks, who have as good a claim to liberty as themselves'. But eleven years later the Constitution of the United States was to declare that 'No person held to service or labor in one State...escaping into another... shall be discharged from such service and labor, but shall be delivered up on the claim of the party to whom such service or labor may be due.' It is true that, in the draft drawn up for Congress for the Declaration of Independence, British permissiveness about the slave trade (as distinct from the institution itself) was roundly condemned, but this judgement failed to get a mention in the final version of the Declaration, and it certainly found no echo in the Constitution. Slavery had not yet become such a big issue in the Protestant conscience, as it was to be on both sides of the Atlantic in the following century.

1 The topic was discussed by Jasper Griffin in the New York Review of Books, 6 May 1999

Left: Inside the old Lutheran church, York County, USA. The sketch, which was drawn in 1800, shows the singing choir, the congregation and officers of the church.

LE CONGRÈS.

8

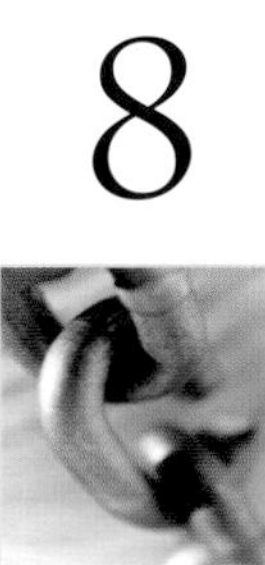

Romantics and Secularists

By 1815, the year of Napoleon's final defeat and of the great peace congress of Vienna that resettled the map of Europe as best it could, the continent had experienced over twenty-five years of wounding wars and revolutions that had torn the old European order to tatters both ideologically and politically. European governments felt they had to pull together to avert the entire collapse of the social order. These feelings had political effects: this was the beginning of the Great Peace in Europe, which lasted until the Crimean War in mid-century.

Russia, which had emerged during the Napoleonic Wars as the new great power, whose influence was no longer confined to the borderlands of Central Europe, was a firm part of what the foreign

Above: The great Kremlin and cathedrals of Moscow, with their distinctive Eastern Orthodox architecture.

Left: A political cartoon showing European leaders celebrating the downfall of Napoleon and the 1815 Congress of Vienna.

Above: The radical English poet Samuel Taylor Coleridge (1772–1834) as a young man.

Below: An illustration of women convicts working in Brixton prison from a study of London prisons by Henry Mayhew (1812–87). Utilitarian Jeremy Bentham had a particular interest in the practical organization of prisons.

ministers called the 'Concert of Europe'. Russian occupying troops were in France in the years immediately following Waterloo, and Russia, representative of the Eastern Orthodox Church, had become quite a powerful influence upon the rest of Christendom. Moscow had been asserted almost from the beginnings of the Russian state as 'new Rome': in a sense the long-defeated forces of Byzantium raised their heads in Europe in the nineteenth century. In the Balkans and Greece, the Hellene and Serb nations asserted themselves against the already centuries-old domination of the Turks.

South America had during the Napoleonic period felt the full effects of the final decline of imperial Spain. By the mid-1820s the whole of South and Central America, barring the islands, had thrown off Spanish or Portuguese allegiance. The churches in Latin America were weakened by the uncertainties of political conflict: the creole, native-born European ruling classes ended by dominating in the whole area. The Church had to follow where they led, sometimes experiencing demoralizing delays. The indigenous populations were always the losers.

A Shift of Ideologies

The Revolutionary and Napoleonic periods had been a time of great political acceleration, in which huge areas of Europe had experienced not only bewilderingly swift changes of rulers, but also equally bewildering shifts of ideologies. The ancient belief systems had suddenly been directly challenged, not only in the cities but also in remote country districts where for hundreds of years the rural masses had known nothing but custom and tradition. The enlightened principles that the privileged classes had ended by more or less accepting, though often without making any real attempt to reconcile them with the religious system that continued to rule large parts of their lives, had displayed volcanic revolutionary potential. The militarization of society had suddenly been carried to a point probably unknown in Europe since the decline of the Roman Empire. National military conscription had previously been practised only in Russia; now under Napoleon it had become the rule in the most civilized country in Europe.

Faced by these challenges and threats, 'Restoration' society tried to repair the ship of the *ancien régime*, which had turned out to be in such a dangerously leaky condition. Publicists and literary folk often tended to swerve to the conservative side. There were still British literary radicals, but the poets Southey and Wordsworth represented a conformist trend. The poet Coleridge was no conformist; he was also one of the most important political philosophers of the century, the main importer into Britain of German philosophical conservatism, that had many implications for the religious outlook.

After 1815 thoughtful people tended to divide between those who consciously rejected the legacy of the eighteenth-century Enlightenment, and were either looking for or promoting a conservative alternative, and those who thought that the political and ethical values of the Enlightenment could be preserved, and that people ought to work for the progressive improvement of society in a constructive and non-revolutionary manner. Great Britain was especially encouraging to radicals of the latter sort, to people such as the philosopher Jeremy Bentham (1748–1831), who were in the last analysis Utopian Radicals, who thought that the rational reorganization of society to achieve the greatest good of the greatest number of citizens could be proceeded with indefinitely, without serious risk of social and political disturbance. Such ideas of what came later to be called 'social engineering' were under one label or another to remain influential in British society for a very long time indeed.

The British had already, in response to the challenges of the French Revolution, produced a political philosopher of great stature in Edmund Burke (1729–97). Burke's genuine traditionalism and respect for archaic custom had little equivalent in continental Europe. Curiously, the critical period of 1815–48, in which most of the ideas that lay behind twentieth-century politics were first elaborated, was one in which the most conservative thinkers were just as revolutionary and just as destructive as declared revolutionaries such as Marx. The innate intellectual conservatism of most of the Enlightenment philosophers, with their reliance on the ideas of natural virtue and natural law, has already been remarked on. Even these philosophies could get politically out of hand, as had happened in France in the last decade of the eighteenth century. But the conservative political philosophies maturing in Germany in Napoleonic times were potentially far more radical, especially in their conception of a kind of national and popular spirit, disembodied but absolutely real, that is permanent and integral to the social body. Such nationalism had terrible potential, even if for a long time it was expressed in terms that made it practically unintelligible to ordinary people.

The extreme conservatism of the French political philosopher Joseph de Maistre (1753–1821) was to some extent couched in religious language. It appeared on the surface to favour the stability of the established order. But when examined closely it was inspired by a sort of savage praise of despotism and irrationalism that included de Maistre's famous panegyric of the executioner, whom he saw as the great protector of civil and religious order. De Maistre has been said to have been in some ways a precursor of twentieth-century Fascism. In theological terms he is much stronger on punishment than on grace: forgiveness was not a word in his vocabulary.

One of the great clashes of the French Restoration period was between believers who saw the Enlightenment as a betrayal of all the values of tradition, understanding tradition in the Christian sense of the doctrine passed down through the grace conferred by the Holy Spirit, and those who (as the traditionalists saw it) to varying degrees allowed themselves to be affected by the spirit of 'liberalism'. This kind of traditionalism was essentially a religious movement led by the clergy, and very different from the innovatory and extreme politics of de Maistre.

In the Church of England the traditionalist movement became known (from its pamphlets published at an early stage) as the 'Tractarian' movement. John Henry Newman (1801–90, converted from Anglicanism to Roman Catholicism in 1845), later Cardinal of the Roman Church, in his account of his religious life as an Anglican defined liberalism in religion as 'the anti-dogmatic principle and its developments'. He described the birth of the Tractarian religious movement of 1833 as due to the sermon preached for Oxford Assizes in that year on 'National Apostasy' by a clergyman who remained firmly Anglican, namely John Keble (1792–1866), a distinguished man who is now better remembered for his hymns than for his doctrines.

The title of Keble's sermon gives some idea of the aggressive and even ferocious character of the Church conflicts of that time.[1] Liberalism, strange as this may sound to modern ears, was viewed by traditionalists as the enemy of all truth, even as the harbinger of antichrist. It is perhaps now especially difficult to see this, because contemporary people are most likely to think of the Tractarian or maybe the 'Puseyite' (from another Tractarian leader, Edward Pusey, 1800–82) movement in the context of the neo-Gothic churches that its clergymen have left behind, rather than in that of the now unfamiliar language of their books and sermons.

The Tractarians, including those among them who 'went to Rome', were characterized by strong

Left: A caricature of the British philosopher Edmund Burke (1729–97). In 1790 he published Reflections on the French Revolution, *which opposed the principles of the Revolution and was read throughout Europe.*

yearning for the Christian Middle Ages, which many of them saw as having been betrayed by the men of the 'enlightened' tendency in the churches. The vogue for medieval paraphernalia and chivalry had already, long before the Romantic-Catholic period, acquired some roots in the eighteenth-century Enlightenment, when the vogue for the neo-Gothic first appeared. It was a taste that could appear and reappear in many forms. The feeling for the lost and regretted Catholic Middle Ages was passed on from the religious right to the great prophet of art and non-dogmatic socialism, John Ruskin (1819–1900), and from Ruskin it went in a lay form to the unbelieving poet and preacher of handicraft and socialism, William Morris (1834–96) – although in the next generation a very different version of Catholic medievalism was also strong in the right-wing writers G. K. Chesterton (1874–1936) and Hilaire Belloc (1870–1953). From Morris the nostalgia was in its secular version transmitted to the twentieth century through the Arts and Crafts Movement. At the end of this century, having picked up a little romantic primitivism on the way, medievalism has found a precarious home in parts of the modern ecological movement. Perhaps we may think of some of this ideological line of descent when we next take our Pevsner guidebooks to view a Puseyite neo-Gothic church, or the Birmingham collection of Pre-Raphaelite paintings.

In spite of the austerities of the lives of the Tractarians and of the Catholic converts, nineteenth-century medievalism formed a link with the arts that was to flourish and endure. There was enormous interest in the study of medieval artefacts after the end of the Napoleonic Wars, and for the rest of the nineteenth century. During the Revolution the iconoclasm of republican France had been so intense that there was danger that the whole patrimony of French medieval church art would disappear. But a refuge for a large number of objects had been found by Alexandre Lenoir, who had set up the Musée des Monuments Français in Paris in 1795, which became, after a shaky start, one of the first of the national museums. After 1815 great lists and catalogues of the medieval artistic repertoire and its monuments were published in several countries: there were both religious and nationalistic aspects to this.

Above: A studio portrait of the British author and art critic John Ruskin.

Below: William Morris, British craftsman, poet and utopian socialist.

One of the great monuments of neo-Gothic enthusiasm in England was a national one, the reconstructed Houses of Parliament in London (1840–60), an enterprise in which the architect Sir Charles Barry was advised on Gothic decoration by A. W. N. Pugin, the son of the theologian. In England in mid-century, while Ruskin was making himself into a national figure, the Pre-Raphaelite painters launched themselves into a sort of learned primitivism, that sought to achieve a return to the condition of painting before its transformation by the supposed classicism of the High Renaissance painters. It was a heterodox movement from a religious as well as from an artistic point of view – Dante Gabriel Rossetti (1828–82), for example, was the son of an anti-clerical Italian revolutionary. Ruskin, while cautious about some of the technical aspects of Pre-Raphaelite work, nonetheless welcomed it as likely to 'lay in England the foundations of a school of art nobler than the world has seen for three hundred years'. In its religious aspects the Pre-Raphaelite paintings of William Holman Hunt (1827–1910), especially, were to make an enormous appeal to the Protestant piety of the time. The

Left: The spectacular ceiling and mosaic of the Central Hall in the Houses of Parliament, London. Re-designed by the architects Pugin and Barry, the Houses of Parliament provide a prime example of the neo-Gothic architecture much loved by Victorians.

Below: The Blind Girl *by artist John Everett Millais (1829–96), one of the founder members of the Pre-Raphaelite Brotherhood.*

most emotive of them all, his *Light of the World*, was painted for the chapel of the Oxford College named after the Tractarian Keble: while working on this in 1851–53 Hunt experienced a religious conversion.

Ideological Choices

Behind all the religious controversies lay an issue that crossed the boundaries of confessions and political trends. How far were believers to defend the status quo, or the traditions of the Church as they understood them, without making any concession to the spirit and the thinking of the times? Were they a rearguard that must die at its post, as the 'ultramontane' Catholic faction of Cardinal Manning (1808–92) (who had his Protestant equivalents), sometimes tended to think? Or were they to view themselves as men of their own day, who looked at the doctrines of other men of their own time in the light of what understanding the Gospel might give them? Newman, in spite of the intransigence of his Tractarian and pre-Catholic days, belonged in a very private and discreet way to the second group rather than the first: his theory of theological development placed him among the ancestors of what came to be known as Catholic modernism. The choice is still not an obsolete one today, even if the terms in which it is put are rather different. But the contrast between traditionalists

Above: The Light of the World *by William Holman Hunt (1827–1919), shows Christ with a lantern knocking at a firmly closed door, symbol of a recalcitrant sinner.*

Right: The stirring image of Liberty Leading the People *painted by the French artist, Eugène Delacroix (1798–1863) after the French Revolution of 1830.*

and modernizers is seldom as stark as it sounds; for example, towards the end of his life Manning experienced a very modern sympathy for the situation of organized workers, a kind of understanding of the industrial world that had passed Newman by.

The test case in early nineteenth-century Catholicism was that of the French priest, Félicité de Lamennais (1782–1854), who had earlier been an admirer of Joseph de Maistre. Having started as a strong 'reactionary', de Lamennais gradually veered round to a position that wanted much more freedom for the Church from the State, even when the State was overtly Catholic. After the July Revolution of 1830, which substituted the 'liberal' Orleanist dynasty on the French throne for its Bourbon cousins, de Lamennais reached a point where he felt that the French Church needed more freedom from the papacy, as well as from the government. His political role changed: he became a liberal publicist who was in principle a democrat advocating the separation of Church and State in France and the recognition of liberty of conscience. He and one or two associates at the end of 1831 made the quixotic gesture of travelling to Rome to put their case before Pope Gregory XVI (pope 1831–46). They were perhaps received more politely than they might have been, because it was known that their requests had wide backing from the Catholics of Belgium and Poland (the Catholic nation that had just rebelled against Russia). But their case was an absolutely hopeless one, both politically and in terms of Church policy. De Lammenais was really asking the Vatican to approve French radicalism and Polish nationalism in the same breath, and it had absolutely no intention of doing either: what is amazing, and creditable to Pope Gregory XVI, is that the pope treated him with such personal courtesy.

Pope Gregory XVI's answer to the Poles came swiftly, with the condemnation of their rebellion against Russia. The pope did not condemn de Lamennais by name when the Vatican acted officially in 1832, but the doctrines Lamennais professed, and other 'modern' doctrines, were condemned generally. Freedom of conscience was described in the papal encyclical not only as a false doctrine, but as a rather insane opinion (delirium). In 1834 Pope Gregory XVI condemned de Lamennais' book, *Paroles d'un Croyant* (Words of a Believer), and from a Vatican point of view the case was closed.

Pope Pius IX (pope 1846–78) had in the first two years of his pontificate enjoyed the reputation of a liberal pope, and for a short time in 1847–48 he went through some of the motions of becoming a constitutional ruler in the papal state. In Church matters there was scarcely any relaxation of ultramontane policies until after his death. The revolutions of 1848, including that in Rome and the papal state, were defeated. But as the second half of the century unfolded, it became increasingly clear that the national and, to some extent, 'liberal' aims of the great European tribes – the Italians and the Germans, particularly – were going to be achieved. Pius IX viewed this with a defiance that was sometimes jaunty, sometimes despairing. In 1864 he issued a 'Syllabus of Errors', that in our terminology could be called the most comprehensively politically incorrect document of the century. Its most provocative denial was the refusal to admit that 'the Roman Pontiff can and should reconcile and harmonize himself with progress, with liberalism, and with recent civilization'.

In 1869, when all Italy outside Rome and its immediate surroundings had already been absorbed, sometimes peacefully but often by force, in the new Piedmontese monarchy of Italy, Pius IX called the First Vatican Council of the Church. It issued its final constitutional decree in the following year on 18 July, the day before the Franco-Prussian War broke out. Decisions of the Roman bishop were declared, when he spoke exercising the office of pastor and teacher of all

Above: Images of child mine-workers from a government report on children's employment dated 1842, the first such report to be illustrated. Atrocious conditions, and the proximity of both sexes to each other, shocked the Victorians.

Right: The industrial landscape of Bolton, Lancashire, in 1848.

Below: Over London, by Rail, *by the French painter Gustav Doré shows graphically the cramped, squalid conditions of Victorian London.*

Christians, and defined doctrine concerning faith and morals to be held by the universal Church, to be infallible [irreformable] in themselves, and not from the consent of the Church. So far as the bishops and cardinals of the council went, their agreement to the infallibility decree was far from unanimous: not less than a quarter of those attending had opposed it in the form in which it was passed. The significance of the decree goes far beyond the nineteenth century, because of its drastic implications for other Christian confessions that may seek to enter into communion with the Roman Church.

On 20 September 1870 the troops of King Victor Emmanuel entered Rome. The papal state's eleven centuries of existence ended, and the Catholic Church had to wait until 1929 before the legal position of its chief bishop in his own house was freely negotiated with the surrounding national state of Italy. The Italian 'Law of Guarantees' of 1871 that regulated the legal position at that time was a unilateral act on the part of the Italian government, which Pius IX rejected. After 1871 the pope was often described as 'the prisoner of the Vatican'.

Industrialism: Socialism: Revolution

In Britain by the early nineteenth century, the new industrial and mining areas were the most conspicuous novel feature of economic and social life. The structures of village life had not been

replaced in the new urban or quasi-urban areas, and this absence of structure extended to the Churches. The new industrial class tended to be ignorant of religion, or yet more ignorant than the old agricultural class, because its ministers were not present to teach or assist them. The same problems applied to the poor areas of the vastly expanded capital cities and great administrative centres, with the difference that very large numbers of the new population were foreigners in one sense or another, very often (like Irish Catholics and Central European Jews in London) belonging to different religions or to different religious groups from the majority culture. The minority religious leaders did their best: Catholic organization in expanding Birmingham, for example, represented a heroic effort. There was, equally, a huge Methodist and Dissenting effort to meet the needs for basic education and moral guidance of what was effectively a displaced population, which in the Methodist case had formed part of the original Wesleyan mission.

Both in Europe and in North America, the established Churches of every persuasion were slow and tepid in their response to this new challenge of the needs of the neglected poor and the disadvantaged workers. Their social attitudes tended to be strongly repressive: the pan-European conservatism of 1815 and its terror of disorder and rebellion were still alive and well. In Catholic Europe the religious orders committed to the poor, not only the Franciscans of medieval origin, but those founded by St Vincent de Paul and others in the Counter-Reformation period, did not possess the structures that were really necessary to deal with the new pastoral problems.

Far from the Vatican, Karl Marx (1818–83) and Friedrich Engels (1820–95) met and formed what was to be a lifelong friendship. In 1845, Engels published *The Condition of the English Working Class*, and the two men collaborated on *The German Ideology*. In Brussels the following year, Marx and other Socialists were pouring out pamphlets; by 1847, they were organized into the Communist League, which, in 1848, issued its declaration of faith, the *Communist Manifesto*, written by Marx. For Marx, religion was the opium of the masses, a drug that was politically administered to them by the rulers.

Marx's revolutionary doctrine was to remain, in spite of its later 'scientific' clothes and its historical paraphernalia, a secular millenarianism that looked forward to a utopian end of history. Christian concern for the poor had always existed, although in the modern period in forms that nineteenth-century Socialists very often found disgusting, and humiliating to the people they were supposed to assist. The issue between the Socialists and the Christian Socialists, when the latter began to come into existence after 1848, was not over means but over ends. The latter wanted to relieve the poor; the former wanted – in modern diction – to empower them.

By contrast, the British liberalism that was classically elaborated by John Stuart Mill (1806–73) was a restatement of many of Bentham's main utilitarian positions, qualified by an assertion of 'the free development of individuality' as one of the main essentials of a citizen's well-being. Mill was particularly strong against 'the engines of moral repression', which he regarded as not merely coming from governments, but from people who try to tyrannize by stigmatizing those whose opinions they think wrong or mistaken, in the court of public opinion. Mill quoted with approval the judgement that his age – one must ask whether the same can be said of our age – was 'destitute of faith, but terrified of scepticism'.

It was difficult for Christians to admit that there could be a political statement of the ultimate end of man: on the other hand, an attitude to the alleviation of social problems could still be taken by Christians, which recognized that part of the bad situation of the workers derived from failure to concede them full political rights. In the English case this trend appeared after 1848 – the year in

Above: Socialist and Communist pamphlets, which were published in large numbers from the mid-1800s. For Marx, religion was the 'opium of the masses'. The established Churches were slow to respond to the needs of the industrial poor and some turned to trade unionism or movements such as Chartism to improve their conditions.

Right: Dock workers on strike in 1889. Towards the end of the nineteenth century there was an upsurge of militancy, particularly among so-called 'unskilled' workers such as dockers and matchgirls.

which Britain was one of the few major European countries not to experience violent revolution – and took the form of accepting a kind of cautious recognition of some of the positions adopted before 1848 by the radical Chartist Party. The leading figure was Frederick Denison Maurice (1805–72), an Anglican theologian from a Unitarian background. Maurice, in combination with the novelist Charles Kingsley (1819–75) and others, termed their new group 'Christian Socialists'. There was very little common ideological ground between the Christian and the secular Socialists, except for a general concern about social issues, which were to become increasingly important to all the major Christian Churches in Europe. In England Cardinal Manning showed himself aware of at least some of the issues, as became apparent from his intervention in one of the London dock strikes.

Later in the century Pope Leo XIII (pope 1878–1903) turned very cautiously in the direction of social-reformist Christianity. In 1888 he allowed that a Catholic might without sin prefer a democratic form of government – the American example was compelling, although later in his pontificate Leo XIII took fright at the democratic contagion that he felt was affecting the Catholic church in North America. With Europe in mind, in 1891 he issued an encyclical, *Rerum novarum*, that, while it asserted the rights of property and condemned Socialism and Communism, recognized that justice might require the state to legislate to protect workers against unjust conditions, and that workers might associate in trade unions to protect their rights, although the same document condemned the strike weapon. Soon after, the first Catholic trade unions began to be formed.

Slavery: a Test Case

One of the greatest victories of the evangelical movement was the abolition of the slave trade. It may legitimately be asked why, after a silence of almost 1,800 years, the Christian conscience should have turned in this direction. Medieval clergy opposed the traffic in Christian slaves by other Christians, but offered no opposition to trafficking in non-Christians. Conversion to Christianity on the part of Christian-owned slaves continued to offer no prospect of manumission, and on the whole the missionaries were anxious to convince slave-owners of this, so that they might offer no opposition to slave Christianization. The Roman bishops had taken up no particular position in the matter, and, as temporal rulers in the mid-sixteenth century, they specifically legalized the ownership of slaves in their own city of Rome.

Enlightenment ideas about human rights did not necessarily lead to opposition to the institution of slavery, as the career of the slave-owning Thomas Jefferson, one of the founding fathers of independent America, shows. In Britain the anti-slavery platform found unlikely champions in the far-from-enlightened precincts of the British common law, when Lord Mansfield (1705–93) decided that slaves enjoyed the status of freedom from their presence on British soil, or even in a ship docked in a British port.

William Wilberforce (1759–1833) was one of a small group of evangelical members of Parliament. He also belonged to a group of influential evangelical laymen and laywomen (later known as the 'Clapham sect', from their place of residence). The committee for the abolition of the slave trade was set up in 1787, relying not only on evangelical sentiment (in fact Quakers were the most numerous sect among its members), but also on the general effect of two propagandist books recently published by ex-slaves under their own names. The books of the West Africans Olaudah Equiano and Ottobah Cugoano recounted their own experiences of captivity. An important part of the first push for abolition had thus come from black Protestant intellectuals, able to tell their own tales and to use the sense of the exotic and alarming to influence their readers.

The government had not been especially enthusiastic about abolition, especially as the French Revolutionary panic, and the brief revolutionary government in Haiti of the black Toussaint l'Ouverture (?1743–1803) from 1794 had made people nervous. But general public pressure had been

Above: Olaudah Equiano, a Protestant, who wrote an account of his own experiences as a slave, which played a major role in informing the abolition movement.

Left: Images such as this of a kneeling slave, entitled Am I Not A Man and a Brother, *were struck on commemorative medallions in the eighteenth century to encourage abolition of the British slave trade.*

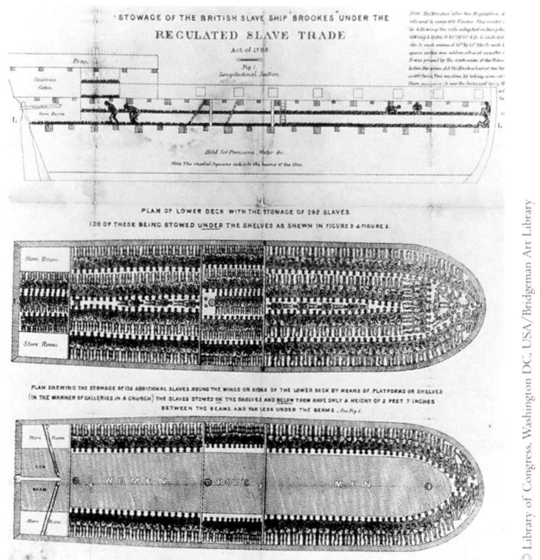

Above: An engraving showing how Africans were packed into slave ships for the transatlantic crossing. The sea trade in humans was lucrative; some 7 million were taken to the Caribbean in the eighteenth century.

strong enough to secure the passing of the Total Abolition of the Slave Trade Act in 1807, and to get it followed up by other legislation that gave the prohibition of the trade some teeth. Nothing less than British naval dominance of the seas could have enabled abolition, and in this the abolitionists were especially fortunate. There was some trouble in getting all the European powers to accept the abolition of the trade in 1815, and even more in pursuing the slavers on the high seas to enforce it. It was a cause that generally attracted at least lip service, rather like some human rights issues in our own time. It is significant that as shrewd a political operator as Napoleon, who as emperor had reintroduced slavery, decided when he had not too much to lose during the Hundred Days of 1815 that it was a good idea to swing to abolition. It was, however, idealism and not calculation that made Pope Gregory XVI condemn the the slave trade in 1839.

A Christian Century?

The nineteenth century was not a century of unbelief: to its end religious issues occasioned passionate concern, and often violent political conflict. In countries such as France, Spain, Germany and Italy, the national State attempted to exercise strict controls over the Church. These could not only affect its freedom to name its own leaders and educate the faithful, including its right to decide how to train its own seminary students, but could also involve huge uncompensated confiscations of Church property. In Britain these conflicts were not entirely absent, but were very much milder: the biggest issues of Church property and policy, for example, had been settled by the end of the seventeenth century, and other less central ones were settled during the nineteenth century, not without fuss, but without the bitter struggles that happened in continental Europe. The religious disquiets of the Victorian liberal intellectuals point in one way, but there were pointers in a different direction. The big effort at church reorganization by the Anglicans and the contemporary dissenting expansion both tried to cope with the change in the industrial and social base. The enormous profusion of church-building also testifies to vitality in the Churches. These things are evidence of the power and vigour of Victorian capitalism no less than of religious zeal, but they are not merely that.

Left: A scene embroidered on to a handkerchief from a series of Illustrations of Missionary Scenes dated c. 1880. Christian missionaries were active worldwide during the nineteenth century, and the scene provides a graphic message.

In the United States the guarantees of the free exercise of religion meant that the clashes of the old world were more or less avoided, although before the emancipation of slaves at the end of the Civil War, in 1865, the blacks did not in practice have the right to organize their own churches. After the Civil War this was one of the few civil rights of self-organization that many blacks in the south of the United States enjoyed, although even this right was frequently contested, and not only in the south. In the north and the west, the great immigrations of the nineteenth and early twentieth centuries meant that the United States remained a Christian country, but became the home of very many Christian confessions, Catholic, Orthodox, and Protestant of every shade and persuasion.

Left: English officers stand at the back of an African congregation in about 1880, looking on while a white minister takes the service. Despite the expansion of Christianity, there was a reluctance on the part of Protestants to encourage or accept indigenous leadership in the churches.

Above: Afro-Americans at the Mount Olive Baptist Church in New York wait to be transported to Liberia, where in the early nineteenth century, a settlement had been created specifically for freed slaves.

Missions

Catholic missionary effort in the world had been centrally directed since 1622 from the Roman Congregation De Propaganda Fide, whose elegant headquarters, designed by Bernini, belied the deadly seriousness and huge scale of the enterprise. The Anglicans had set up the basic structures of missionary effort abroad at the end of the seventeenth century, when Thomas Bray (1656–1730) had founded the Society for the Propagation of Christian Knowledge (SPCK) in 1698, and backed it up in the following year by the Society for the Propagation of the Gospel in Foreign Parts (SPG). A further central organization, the Church Missionary Society, was added under evangelical inspiration in 1799 by the efforts of the biblical commentator, Thomas Scott (1747–1821).

The world expansion of Christianity during the nineteenth century was huge. Colonization was everywhere accompanied, sometimes preceded, by missionary effort. The impulse among the missionaries was sometimes humanitarian, sometimes strongly colonialist. There was a great reluctance among Protestants to acknowledge indigenous leadership in African churches; the only exceptions were in the colonial settlement of Sierra Leone, set up in the late eighteenth century for repatriated and freed slaves, and the later American-founded settlement of Liberia in the early nineteenth century, made for the same purpose.

Everywhere the confessional differences among the missionaries corresponded more or less to the colonial interests of the great European powers. That it was possible to serve both France and the Church in the mission field was freely – for example – asserted. On the other hand, Catholic missionary work in Africa very often antedated European colonialism by some centuries, and the popes constantly insisted with the religious missionary orders, throughout the nineteenth century and into the twentieth, that it was the duty of Catholic missionaries to respect local cultures, to avoid serving national interests, and to create an indigenous clergy. These precepts were to some extent observed by the Catholic clergy, but were a great deal less present, at all events in the high tide of nineteenth-century colonial expansion, to the minds of the Protestants.

Science, Religion, and the Higher Criticism

From Wesley to Newman, the disquiet of the troubled soul had been responsible for great changes in the faith, for trends towards rebirth and revival. But later in the nineteenth century, for the first time since such movements as the Gnosticism and Manichaeism of antiquity, the troubled Christian spirit began once more to cross thresholds that led away from the faith altogether. That was one of the factors in ethical liberalism, that in Britain had earlier been contained by the very English phenomenon of late Unitarianism, but that in the later nineteenth century was to lead numbers of very sensitive and civilized intellectuals, of whom the novelist George Eliot (1819–80) is a distinguished example, away from the churches into a world of ideas and ideals in which allegiances were very much harder to distinguish. The phenomenon was defined by Matthew Arnold (1822–88), in his poem, 'Dover Beach', written soon after his marriage to Frances Lucy Wightman in 1851, in which the metaphor of the tide retreating from the shore was memorably used of the retreat from faith:

> *...The Sea of Faith*
> *Was once, too, at the full, and round earth's shore*
> *Lay like the folds of a bright girdle furled.*

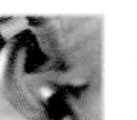

But now I only hear
Its melancholy, long, withdrawing roar,
Retreating, to the breath
Of the night-wind, down the vast edges drear
And naked shingles of the world.

Ah love, let us be true
To one another ! for the world, which seems
To lie before us like a land of dreams,
So various, so beautiful, so new,
Hath really neither joy, nor love, nor light,
Nor certitude, nor peace, nor help for pain;
And we are here as on a darkling plain
Swept with confused alarms of struggle and flight,
Where ignorant armies clash by night.

The pessimism of the second of these stanzas, and its suggestion that the forces of nature are indifferent to man's plight, indicate a sadness that was to be typical of one branch of the doubting Victorians. There is no pleasure in this flight to doubt, no roll of drums in honour of the advancing forces of reason. To describe the human predicament when the tide of faith had withdrawn, the metaphors chosen are those of conflict and desolation. Arnold's was a very Christian doubt.

In continental Europe the markers had to a large extent been laid down in the Enlightenment and the French Revolution, so that the ideological emphasis in the nineteenth century was on the construction of tools with which to achieve social aims that were, at the minimum, of betterment, at the maximum, utopian. In this process the Church was assigned no role, unless an obstructive one that required its removal.

Most of the lines of thought that took shape later in the century, either in the social philosophy of positivism, or in various strands of Socialism, are to be found in the extraordinary French thinker, Henri de Saint-Simon (1760–1825). The thought of Saint-Simon was historicist, anti-egalitarian, technocratic and managerial: he could see the existence of a class war, but planned for its removal. He wished for the social control of both man and nature by a new rational order, scientific and authoritarian. He condemned the whole Church and State apparatus of the *ancien régime* as obsolete and useless. To settle the new technocratic regime he wanted the establishment of a new religion – and in the 1830s some Saint-Simonian churches were in fact set up in France.

Above: The Brtish novelist George Eliot (Mary Ann Evans).

Above: A cartoon from 1861 showing Charles Darwin with an ape-like body sitting next to an ape, both noting their common features in a mirror. It was this aspect of Darwin's theories that caused such controversy.

Saint-Simon's thought was too complicated and inconsistent to get the attention of more than a restricted circle of intellectuals, but his disciple Auguste Comte (1798–57) was important in changing the climate of opinion. Comte, like his master and like Lenin, was convinced that applied science would satisfactorily deal with all our problems, social and otherwise. His philosophy of 'positivism' applied to itself the concept of 'inevitability', a sort of apotheosis that was to be gratefully seized upon by Marxism. Because Comte had a great gift for simplification and presentation, he became for a very large number of educated Europeans and Americans a kind of prophet of the inexorable victory of the scientifically planned society. Like his master, he required the new order to be founded on a new religion, which he termed the 'religion of humanity'. It was all a bit thin, and somewhat authoritarian, and George Eliot, among many other thoughtful people, found it so.

Two main forces were publicly and widely acknowledged as the main agencies in the weakening of Christian belief. One, of which much has already been said above, was the criticism of religion that alleged its own 'scientific' basis. The other, which was really a sub-category of the first, was the 'scientific' criticism applied by biblical critics to the scriptural texts.

The latter was a department in which there had been plenty of Enlightenment precursors and some pre-Enlightment ones: the most destructive remained Spinoza. In the late nineteenth century much of the most important textual work on the Scriptures was carried out, not with the destructive aim of weakening the faith, but with the apologetic one of defending it. And it is possible that in Protestant countries, where for centuries the whole weight of Church preaching had been upon the word of God, the most disturbing knowledge was not that of the discovery of particular details in the scriptural texts that went ill with traditional emphases, but the knowledge that such enquiry was going on at all. 'Historical criticism', as it came to be known, found acceptance more easily among the churchmen who knew that its purpose was benign, than among the laymen who found it threatening.

When scholars talked about the Jesus of history, as they began to do near the end of the century, they usually meant that they were trying to deal with the history of Jesus by roughly the same scholarly methods that they would have applied to any other topic of the history of his time. The same limits on our understanding therefore apply to him, if he is looked at in this way, that would apply to anyone else. The Jesus that seemed to emerge from their work was still in many ways the loved and loving teacher, but some things about him had become disturbingly uncertain, or unfamiliar. To this extent the higher criticism was genuinely disquieting to faith.

Whether these theological doubts (if things so general can be called that) were the most potent solvent of Christian belief, or whether this priority had to be given to the great quarrels of 'science and religion' was a matter much discussed at the time. Mrs Humphrey Ward (1851–1920), the niece of Matthew Arnold, in her novel *Robert Elsmere* (1888), decided that the priority belonged to the higher scriptural criticism. But enormous publicity had attended the publication of Darwin's *On the Origin of Species* in 1859, and his subsequent very public confrontation at the meeting of the British Association for the Advancement of Science in 1860 with Bishop Wilberforce, who was a scientist.

Darwin's thesis had two quite different aspects so far as orthodox belief was concerned. On the one hand, he asserted, in a by no means revolutionary way so far as the science of his time was concerned, the validity of geological time. Biblical time, in so far as it was based on the chronology that appeared to be given in the text of Old Testament, had still preoccupied the old age of Newton: it could not possibly be fitted into the enormously long timescale that the new geology required. However, the most significant part of Darwin's thesis was not geological time, although it was necessary to it. Darwin's theories were a genuine scientific revolution, but they attracted public attention not because of the power of his abstract thought but because of the label of 'descent from apes' that was attached to them. They were only worrying to theologians if a dogmatic positivist philosophy was appended, and although plenty of contemporary positivists welcomed Darwinism, Darwin was not himself a positivist.

In the last part of the century there was a substantial body of combative rationalism that saw itself with a duty to attack and subvert the Christian faith. It was atheistic rather than agnostic, positivist in tendency. Polemicist Winwood Reade's rather breathlessly aggressive *Martyrdom of Man* (1872) contained an attempt at a rationalist philosophy of history that lacked the depth and reflective breadth that were needed for the enterprise, although there is a kind of poetic fervour to the book that impresses. He made quasi-religious claims: 'The religion that I teach is as high above Christianity as that religion was superior to the idolatry of Rome'. But his conclusion was not far from that of Matthew Arnold, twenty years earlier:

'A season of mental anguish is at hand, and through this we must pass in order that our posterity may rise. The soul must be sacrificed; the hope in immortality must die. A sweet and charming illusion must be taken from the human race, as youth and beauty vanish never to return.'

'Mental anguish' perhaps best describes the plight of the doubting Victorians. It was to take another century before doubt could become orthodox and comfortable. Religious doubt was over a long period going to lead towards a new secular morality, and social reform was the main path to lead in this direction. Gradualist Socialism was not a new religion, but it was an ethical attitude that helped to push religion out of its former dominant place in social morality. Beatrice Webb, one of the two great architects of Socialist Fabianism, and co-author of *Soviet Communism: A New Civilization?* was going to define this shift in her autobiography:

'...it was during the middle decades of the nineteenth century that in England, the impulse of self-subordination was transferred, consciously and overtly, from God to man...'.

1 There is an unusual feeling for this in the Cambridge historian Maurice Cowling's *Religion and Public Doctrine in Modern England (Cambridge, 1981-5)*

9

VIOLENCE AND DOUBT

Like so many centuries before it, the twentieth has been a time of ruthless and relentless violence. That this should have been so has been no surprise to many conservative Christians, nor, in principle, to many conservative Jews, although the planned violence that overwhelmed the Jewish communities of continental Europe in the Hitler period had no precedent in a history that already contained many terrible acts committed against them. It was also a century in which Christians almost certainly suffered no less persecution than under the Roman Empire.

Two world wars, including the unveiled threat of nuclear war with which the second ended, have inflicted grave blows both to the optimism that inspired so much Western secular rationalism in the half-century that preceded 1914, and to the general confidence in human progress in both moral and material matters, that had become integral to the whole culture of the industrialized world. Technology has continued its triumphal march; belief in moral progress perhaps still lingers among us. But injustice and terror, in spite of the great political changes in the former Soviet Union, are far from having finished with us.

Christendom has declined in the West. The idea of many nations constituting a people of God called Christendom, who know and acknowledge their Christian identity, and who have a sort of collective presence in large areas of the planet, has become

Above: War graves at Saint-Laurent-sur-Mer.

Left: Unveiling a War Memorial at Cookham *by Stanley Spencer (1891–1959).*

unfamiliar to most of the populations of the so-called First World. One way of putting this is that the principle of nationality has prevailed over the collective idea of Christianity, although there are cases such as those of Poland or Serbia where the two coincide, or have done until very recently. In most of the countries that once constituted 'Christendom' the proportion of persons who identify themselves clearly as Christians has declined sharply since the beginning of the century.

These things do not point clearly to the decline of Christianity as a world religion. To those who want to take a statistical view of morality the religion has not declined in world terms. It has declined in Europe, where it has returned to being in some countries to what it was in its early centuries – a minority religion with only weak support among the cultural and political élites. In First World democratic countries it is not persecuted, but in the course of the century Christians have in some places and at some times undergone persecution fully as severe as their predecessors experienced under the pagan Roman Empire. The minority situation is new in the very long European history of the religion, or new after the barbarian conversions of the early Middle Ages. It would be far too much to say that it has taken it back to conditions that preceded the conversion of Constantine in the fourth century, because the tenacity of institutions and mental habits means that traditional Christianity is much more widely present among us than we commonly realize. Getting a more precise idea of what this means is like trying to sketch a landscape from a moving train.

Below: French propaganda postcard reflecting the nationalist stance of the Christian Churches during World War I.

World Wars: Fascist and Communist Ideologies

In most of the main Christian countries that took part on either side in the First World War, the main local Christian churches of both Eastern and Western Christianity took a nationalist line. The connection between national Church and national struggle may have been especially strong in Britain, but many people who grew up between the wars were most conscious of the Church in its role as custodian of the memories of the war dead. During the war the Churches had not favoured Christian 'absolute' pacifism: that was confined to a few numerically small sects such as Quakers and Mennonites. Many ministers and priests fought: it was noticeable that the camaraderie that still remained among ex-combatant pastors from the trenches of 1914–18 was a factor in enabling Adolf Hitler to set up a pro-Nazi Protestant Church in 1933–4.

The Roman Catholic Church, under the leadership of Pope Benedict XV (pope 1914–22) took a humanitarian and peace-loving stance that endeared it to neither side. Pope Benedict protested against the inhuman methods of warfare used, such as poison gas, and in August 1917 launched a peace plan. The plan was entirely unacceptable to the Allies, who at that moment enjoyed military advantages they had bought at great human and material cost. It was at first cautiously welcomed by the Central Powers, but then abandoned by them when the internal collapse of Russia seemed to offer them another chance.

The peace plan offered to the combatants by Pope Pius XII (pope 1939–58) in 1939 was couched much more generally, but in fact it contained the main principles of the eventual new international post-war order (equal rights to life and national independence; a new international institution; attention to demands of racial minorities). His plan was disregarded by the combatants on either side. There was a mild and cautious attempt to draw attention to it by Cardinal Hinsley and, on the Anglican side, by Bishop Bell, but that was not the mood in Britain in 1940. It is to be regretted that the pope's other two principle – general disarmament and the recognition of the life of the spirit – did not get the attention of the victorious powers in 1945.

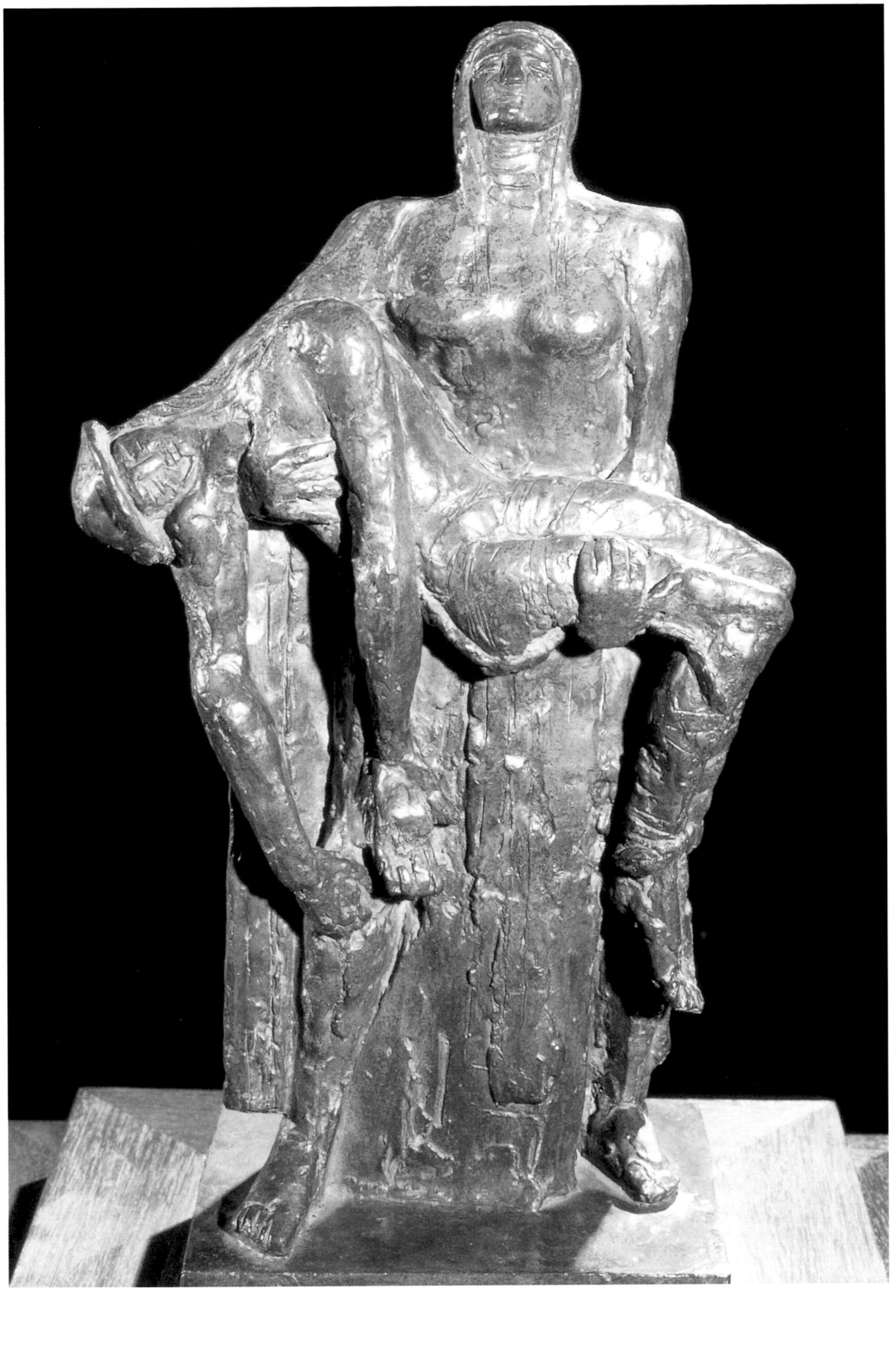

© Bolton Museum and Art Gallery, Lancashire, UK/Bridgeman Art Library

© AKG London

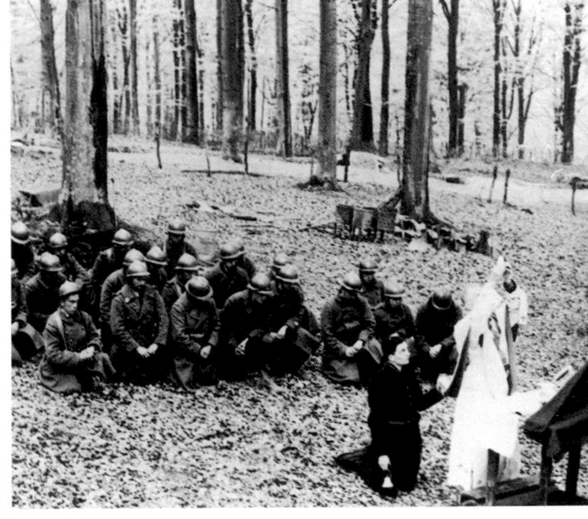

Above: A field service held for French troops just behind the battle lines during World War I. Many members of the clergy saw active service at the front.

Left: Maquette of a war memorial by Jacob Epstein (1880–1959). It was commissioned by the Trades Union Council, to commemorate the sacrifice of many of their members.

Few people had initially understood the grave problems that were to be presented to the Christian conscience by the victories of Fascist governments in the period between the wars, partly because those governments were initially so skilful in concealing the implications their doctrines had for the faith, partly because Fascist hostility to atheist Communism was accepted by many Christians as an indication that in some respects they stood on the same side as the Church. In Spain, the Fascist government enjoyed the open support of the Catholic Church; its authoritarian claims, although considerable, were much fewer than those made in Germany.

Among the more conspicuous of Hitler's dupes was Pope Pius XI (pope from 1922–39), who was tricked into thinking that because he had successfully negotiated a Church concordat with Mussolini (whom he in some respects understood) in 1929, a different sort of concordat could be satisfactorily negotiated with Hitler, whom he did not understand at all. The most skilful Church diplomat of his age was deceived in this way, and he was only sharing the same fate as many European politicians. Understanding of the moral issues presented by Nazi totalitarianism was reserved to others, notably, on the Catholic side, the German Cardinal Faulhaber, and on the Protestant side, the young German pastor, Dietrich Bonhoeffer (1906–45).

Right: Pope Pius XI, duped by Hitler, with Hermann Goering, Hitler's right-hand man, in 1933. They met to discuss the signing of a concordat between the Vatican and the Third Reich.

The German Catholic episcopate had, in fact, taken something of the measure of National Socialism by 1930, and had condemned it in absolutely definite terms. The importance of the Catholic Centre Party in German politics made it very important to the ex-Catholic Hitler somehow to outflank the German Catholic hierarchy, as he finally approached the seizure of power in 1933. He did this by letting it be known in Rome that he was willing to negotiate a Church concordat – never before offered by any national German government – on terms that conceded some of the main issues that he knew were important to the Vatican. The price was the depoliticizing of German Catholicism. Pope Pius XI took the bait, thus abandoning both the German bishops and the Centre Party to the wolves – but not before the Centre Party had consented to the fatal Enabling Law in the Reichstag that became the constitutional basis of the Nazi totalitarian regime.

Left: Book burning and the Nazi salute, chilling images from the time of Hitler's ascent. It was not only art and literature by persons considered to be 'degenerate' that were destroyed; anything unbiased or not actively supporting the Nazi philosophy was also thrown on the bonfire.

In Germany in 1933 the Protestant Churches were overtaken by a whirlwind that they, too, could hardly understand. With the speed and ruthlessness that characterized everything he did, Hitler had his regime set up a new 'German Christian' Church that (by contrast with the regional German Protestant Churches) was organized on a national basis, and that repudiated such 'Jewish' Christian elements as the Old Testament and the writings of St Paul. At the same time the first great Jewish persecution was launched, to exclude Jews from public life, and the German pastorate was to be required to give its assent to these doctrines. Almost alone at first, Dietrich Bonhoeffer realized the central importance of the Jewish racial issue for the Church. Although he allowed the capacity of the state to legislate, Bonhoeffer took the traditional Lutheran position, and wrote that the Church:

> *'recognizes the absolute necessity for the use of force in this world, and also the moral injustice of certain concrete acts of the state which are necessarily bound up with the use of force.'*[1]

But he then showed, by an extraordinary leap, ability to push his thought further and to write that the Church should continually ask whether the actions of the state are such as to lead to law and order, and not to lawlessness and disorder. This must have been a reference to the requirement for legal government, a *Rechtsstaat*, that was fundamental in modern German history. Bonhoeffer was at this very early stage already looking for some kind of critique for a right of resistance to the state: it was a path that was to take him to a Nazi scaffold in 1945 and to make him one of the major figures in twentieth-century Christian history. He again showed his prescience in 1934, when rearmament was only just beginning to be an issue, at the international oecumenical Christian meeting on the Danish North Sea island of Fanø. At that meeting he made the then rather untimely-sounding appeal to:

Above: Pastor Dietrich Bonhoeffer, opposer of Nazi doctrine, who was executed for his defiance on 9 April 1945 at Flössenburg (Bavaria).

Above: Part of the aftermath of the notorious Kristallnacht *('Night of Broken Glass', 9-10 April 1938) when the Nazi militia attacked Jewish homes, shops and synagogues throughout Germany and Austria in a concerted operation. This is the devastated interior of the Okel Jaakov synagogue in Munich.*

'issue to those who believe in Christ a radical call for peace. The hour is late. The world is choked with weapons and dreadful is the mistrust that looks out of all mens' eyes. The trumpets of war may blow tomorrow. For what are we waiting ?'

Bonhoeffer's was a lonely voice, and his close British Church contacts (of whom the most important was George Bell, Bishop of Chichester, whose conscience was a thorn in Churchill's side during the Second World War) did not inspire confidence. It seemed to many prudent conservative Christians in Germany during 1933–4 that the best thing was to recognize the nationalism that many of them shared to a certain degree with the National Socialists, and beyond that not to say too much about politics. Cardinal Faulhaber, on the other hand, asserted the Old Testament in a way that repudiated the Nazi assertion of blood and race as possible elements in Christianity, and that also strikingly held out a hand to the German Protestants (an unheard-of thing for a cardinal to do in 1933), to 'defend with them the sacred books of the Old Testament'. He said, 'We are not saved by German blood. We are saved by the blood of our crucified Lord.' What was in store for German Catholicism became clear only six months later, when on 30 June 1934 the Nazi murderers, who had a lot of work to do that day, walked into the office of the Catholic Action leader, Erich Klausener, and shot him, cynically arranging the murder so that it could be said to have been a suicide. The concordat had been signed eleven months earlier, on 20 July 1933. It took Pope Pius XI several years to realize how thoroughly Hitler had deceived him; eventually, and far too late in the day, in March, 1937 he expressed his disappointment and grief in the encyclical *Mit Brennende Sorge* (With burning concern).

Right: Cloth patch emblazoned with the Star of David and the German word for Jew. Hitler made it compulsory for all Jewish people over the age of six in Germany, Austria and Poland to wear the yellow star so they could be easily identified.

In April 1934 the German evangelical Churches reorganized, in the face of what they had come to realize was a clerical part of the Nazi seizure of power, and formed, against the state-controlled and Nazi-dominated German Christian Church, the Confessing Church, which described itself as the legitimate evangelical Church of Germany. It was one of the few open gestures of resistance to the Nazi takeover in Germany, although it was very careful to declare its allegiance to the state. The

Below: 'Jew-baiting' in Nazi Austria. Jewish shops and services in Vienna were closed down by the Nazis after Kristallnacht *in 1938.*

Left: A twentieth-century icon showing the royal family of Tsar Nicolai II (1895–1917). The link between the Russian Orthodox Church and the Russian monarchy was indissoluble. The downfall of the aristocracy in Russia meant the end of established religion.

Above: What People used to Fight for and What People Fight for Now, *a revolutionary poster by Dmitri Stakhievich Moor, showing how the Church and the monarchy had been replaced by the State and the people.*

Confessing Church survived precariously in the open until war broke out in 1939. The ex-submarine commander Martin Niemöller (1892–1984), the key leader of the Confessing Church movement, was sent to a concentration camp in 1937, and remained there until the end of the war, but miraculously survived the experience, which some other imprisoned Protestant pastors, besides Bonhoeffer, failed to do.

The kind of diplomatic calculation shown by Pope Pius XI in his dealings with Hitler remained in the mentality of the Roman curia under his successor. Pope Pius XII, because of his fear that frankness on his part about the threat to European Jews would make their plight even worse, chose diplomatic inactivity during the critical period of the Jewish massacres. It was a timidity that gained him a subsequent reputation, perhaps only partly deserved, for indifference.

In Soviet Russia the Church suffered one of the greatest persecutions. In the final period of imperial Russia the Orthodox lay intelligentsia, who were predominantly, but not exclusively, Slavophile, but various and creative in their thought, had made a big intellectual contribution, which after 1917 so far as it continued, continued only in exile. This was a tradition of which the writer Solzhenitsyn, who for a long time refused exile, later became a distinguished representative. In post-revolutionary Russia there were very many executions of the clergy, some public, most of them acts of terrorist power. The 1930s saw another wave of persecution and martyrdom, although by that time the clerical structures had been almost entirely destroyed. Anti-God museums and anti-religious instruction became the norm. The huge architectural patrimony of the Russian Orthodox Church came near to destruction. The monasteries as monastic communities simply disappeared. A few bishops survived, under very close state supervision. When the huge size of the old Russian empire is considered, the scale on which these things occurred is breathtaking. There was only a very partial and small relaxation of the stifling hold of state Communism, when the Russian Orthodox clergy were found to be useful by the ex-seminarist, Joseph Stalin, in mobilizing patriotic feeling in the war with Germany, after 1941.

The Cold War and its Contradictions

In the long, discouraging years of the Cold War (1947–89) the persecution of the Churches was extended to the whole area of Europe that lay under Russian leadership and domination. Everywhere east of a new long border that stretched from the Baltic to the southern Adriatic seas, the Churches in varying ways and in varying degrees suffered the most severe disabilities. There were martyrdoms, especially in Albania and Yugoslavia: Tito's post-war regime had, in any case, begun with a most fearful bloodbath. In the Soviet Union itself, and especially in the Ukraine, the old persecutions continued, sometimes with the addition of new victims such as the Protestant sect of the Jehovah's Witnesses (Watchtower Movement) and the Mormons (Latter-Day Saints).

After 1919 a phenomenon had reappeared in European, and eventually in world politics, that had last bedevilled Europe at the time of the seventeenth century Wars of Religion: the tendency to transform political conflicts into religious ones. There was a fatal temptation to turn the political struggle between the new Soviet Union and the conservative powers into a religious struggle between Christian belief and Communist atheism. It was a temptation that Communism itself had aided and abetted, principally by conceiving of itself as an international ideological and political force. Both the Republican and the Nationalist sides in the Spanish Civil War, for example, had very much to answer for in this respect – not only in a general sense but in terms of useless bloodshed. The revival of the ideas of the medieval Crusade could only be harmful, in the end, to a modern Christianity that on the whole wanted to get rid of many of the theological concepts that lay behind the Crusade. These things left long and terrible shadows across the world, which could still be seen as late as the Vietnam War.

One of the most divisive effects of the crusading spirit was a decree of the Holy Office (that is, the former Roman Inquisition) of 1949, confirmed by Pope Pius XII, which ruled that Communion could not be given in the Catholic Church to anyone who subscribed to the Communist

Above: Damage done to the Church of the Twelve Apostles in Moscow after the 1917 Revolution in Russia.

Below: The Berlin Wall, built in under a week in August 1961, blocked off the entrance to the Church of Redemption in Bernauerstrasse, consigning it to the eastern sector.

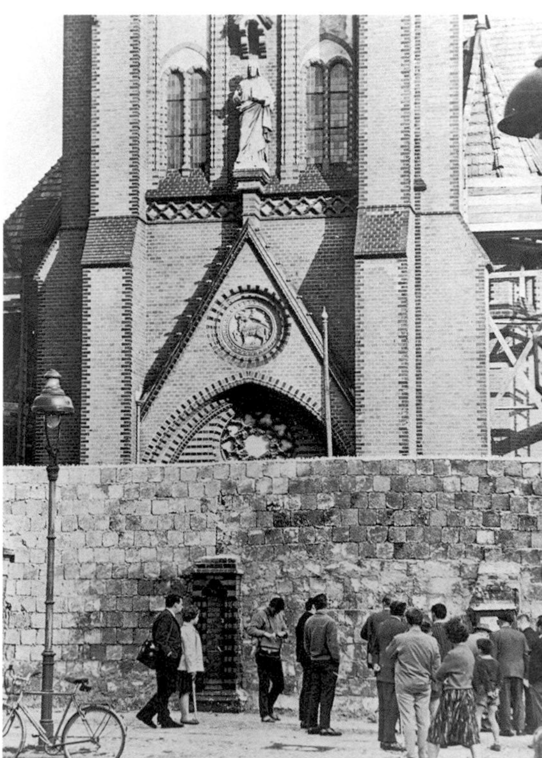

Left: Photograph made in 1970 by Marc Chaimowicz based on the Song-My massacre in Vietnam. The change in attitude to conflict since the start of the century was reflected in the public protests against the war in Vietnam.

Party or publicly advocated Communism. The decree did not say that excommunication followed for anyone who voted in democratic or undemocratic elections for the Communist Party, but it still had serious results in further politicizing the Catholic Church in Western Europe, and in further disadvantaging the position of the faithful in Eastern Europe. It also failed to take account of the position of the many believers who were troubled by the accumulation of nuclear weapons in the world: the decree tended to isolate from the Church those who took part in peace movements, which were often sponsored by the Left, and to accentuate the tendency to classify them as 'fellow-travellers' with Communism.

It occurred to practically no one in those days that before the end of the century Marxist doctrines might be moribund. Another known danger to freedom of conscience, ascendant in the 1930s, but apparently defeated in 1945, has, unlike Marxism, survived triumphantly. Right through the Cold War, the hidden issue was that of nationalism, which the Soviet Union suppressed in Eastern Europe in the name of Communism, just as the Russian government had suppressed it in the first half of the nineteenth century in the name of the conservative Holy Alliance. The Janus face of nationalism that looks at liberty from one side and at oppression from the other has been unchanging since the nineteenth century.

Nationalism can also fuse with religious particularism. The distinguished British church historian, Owen Chadwick, has recorded how the revival of a degree of Serbian government benevolence towards the Orthodox Church began in 1981 with the Albanian destruction of the historic Serbian monastery at Peć, and with the recital by the clergy of a long history of such acts against the Orthodox Church for which Albanians had been responsible in the province of Kosovo[2]. In the history of successful resistance to Soviet rule in Eastern Europe and of the disintegration of the old Warsaw Pact we have to give Polish nationalism an honoured place, just as we have to give Hungarian and Czech nationalism due honour for the parts they played in 1956 and 1968. But it is foolish to forget the debit side of the nationalist sheet, so evident in the break-up of Yugoslavia, that is light for many European nations of the post-Cold War period, especially under the influence of EEC Europeanism, but can still suddenly become heavy. Nationalism has been evident on both sides in Northern Ireland, and has left only a legacy of tears.

The Christian Oikumene

The Greek expression *oikumene* means the inhabited world, which in the days of the still universalist, but Christianized Roman Empire was taken to mean 'the universal Church'. It therefore tends to be an inclusive term, much more than Christendom, which historically has tended to be exclusive. The oecumenical councils of the Church, therefore, were those which represented the whole Church of the *oikumene*. It would be vain, however, to pretend that the *oikumene* could not also have signified the Romano-Hellenic world in opposition to external 'barbarians'. The expression did not signify 'all men', and the theological disputes of the past, whether or not Christ died for 'all men', confirm it. If we say today that Christendom is in decline, and that the oecumenical concept within Christianity is in the ascendant, we are talking about ideological and theological tendencies and not about social facts. Within the past century the oecumenical movement has come to mean, as it previously did not mean, working together for the unity of all who call themselves Christians.

The oecumenical movement has a long and complex history, mainly concerned with the Protestant Churches, but also including early contacts of some of these (mainly the Anglicans) with the Roman Catholics and with the Orthodox – the institutional relevance of the Orthodox to the Anglicans goes back at least to the eighteenth century, when Anglicans were concerned with Orthodox help in ordaining bishops to the new American Episcopalian Church. The World Council of Churches was set up in 1948. By 1998 the number of Churches involved, most but by no means all of which were Protestant, had risen to 335, coming from over a hundred countries and every continent. The Roman Catholic Church, which is itself an group of associated Churches, does not take a direct part in the World Council, but since Vatican II (1962–65, see below) various kinds of Catholic participation in the organization have developed. The ramifications of the oecumenical movement are considerable, especially in the form of regional and confessional groups of Churches.

Before 1962, the date of the convening of the Second Vatican Council (Vatican II) by Pope John XXIII (pope 1958–63), it could have been said, with some reservations, that the oecumenical movement was primarily a phenomenon of the Protestant and Orthodox communities. In order to work to set up Vatican II Pope John established a Secretariat for Promoting Christian Unity, whose duty to help to restore unity among Christians was confirmed when it became a permanent part of the restructured Roman curia in 1989. Vatican II was a critical period for the modern Roman Catholic Church, but in a sense it was also critical for the other main Church groups, which were not only directly affected by its decision to stay in touch with them and to treat them as Churches in a real sense, but were also greatly affected by its thinking and its policies. When the conservative Anglican bishop, Hensley Henson, wrote an affectionately teasing letter to Bishop Bell of Chichester in 1940 about Bell's oecumenical tendencies, he said that Bell seemed to be a spiritual acrobat riding the three horses of Quakerism, Papistry, and up to date Communism.[3] Taken in a very general and imprecise way, especially as to the last term, the observation could be applied to much of the oecumenical movement today.

Another critical opening provided by Vatican II was the decree on religious liberty. It may today seem that the affirmation of the right to freedom of religious conscience is such an obvious and fundamental matter that the Catholic Church should not have experienced the slightest hesitation or delay in making it. That this was not so was not merely due to the Counter-Reformation tradition in the Catholic Church, nor to the overhang of the mentality of the Inquisition. It seemed to many of the Fathers at Vatican II that they were not free to assert the right to affirm error: the existence of the Church depends upon the affirmation of the right tradition, and the evidence for this can be found in its history from apostolic times. At the Second Vatican Council the acceptance of such a decree was politically due to the alliance between the democratic American bishops on one hand and of the clergy from Communist-controlled Europe on the other: memories of the persecution of the Church in Germany and elsewhere by the Nazis, and the Christian failure to offer successful resistance to the Nazi racist laws were also factors.

Below: Pope Paul VI at the start of his historic visit to the Holy Land in 1964.

© Hulton Getty/London

The right to liberty of conscience has always had to be qualified by the reservation that the affirmation of such liberty cannot be allowed to infringe the essential freedoms of others. This is a classical dilemma of liberalism, which the council met by the appeal to natural law. Bishop de Smedt of Bruges argued in 1963 in the same way that Bonhoeffer, confronted by the same problem in 1933 had argued, namely, that imposing the rule of the common good was the business of the state and should not allow people to go against the order of justice established by God.

Pope Paul VI (pope 1963–78) loyally continued the work of his predecessor, Pope John XXIII, and saw the Vatican Council through to its end. Besides the decrees just mentioned, the Council passed another concerning the Jews that referred to a spiritual patrimony that Christians hold in common with Jews. It stated that the Passion of Christ cannot be levelled against all the Jews, thus making the ancient charge of deicide against a whole religion and a whole people unsustainable by Catholic Christians. Vatican II also affirmed that the 'relationship between Jews and Christians concerns the Church as such', which made a continuing concern for that relationship the religious responsibility of all Catholics. The follow-up from these principles received public affirmation in the 1993 agreement between the Holy See and the State of Israel, which established diplomatic recognition of the State of Israel on the part of the Vatican. However, the long space of time that elapsed between Vatican II and the 1993 agreement was due to the continuing and ancient problems of relationships between the two religions, as well as the caution of Vatican diplomats.

One especially significant act of Paul VI was his visit to the Holy Land in 1964 to meet the Orthodox Patriarch of Constantinople, the Senior Orthodox bishop, in Jerusalem, where the two agreed to make the symbolic gesture of cancelling the anathemas imposed by each Church upon the other in 1054, a promise executed in 1965. There were further meetings between the two. In 1980, Pope John Paul II (pope from 1978) and the Orthodox Patriarch Dimitrios I set up the structures for an extended dialogue between the two groups of Churches, which has continued into the present decade.

In more recent times the emphasis has shifted to Christian relations with non-Christian religions other than Judaism, principally with Islam. In Europe, particularly, where large Muslim minorities exist, a big effort has been made to set up institutions of Christian religious and social co-operation with Islamic groups in most major EEC countries. In some countries, particularly the UK, these institutions have extended their activities to include other non-Christian religions, especially those of the Indian sub-continent.

Human Rights and Social Equality

The principles of human rights are enshrined in the United Nations Declaration of Human Rights of 1948, which includes the assertion of religious liberty, and the International Covenants adopted in 1966. Human rights are also protected in various regional agreements, such as those adopted within the European Convention on Human Rights in 1950.

The principles of non-discrimination between social and ethnic groups may be seen as stemming from the main human rights principles, but in practice most of these are enshrined in various bodies of national legislation. This means, of course, that such rights are not enforceable in all countries, and the manner in which they are enforceable in those countries that have the appropriate legislation varies considerably. There are enormous differences between the social philosophies that lie behind, say, the sex-discrimination laws of Great Britain and the United States, and the manner in which such legislation is discussed in Third World countries.

Very broadly, the Anglo-Saxon philosophy that lies behind such laws is one of individual rights. The way in which such things are discussed in the Third World refers much more to collective rights, and to their infringement by other collectivities such as international companies which have oppressive marketing or purchasing practices in Third World areas, or that profit from the continued exaction of interest payments from Third World countries. In other words, bad social conditions in the Third World, including, for example, the poor state of women's rights, are attributed above all to

© Hulton Getty/London

Above: A Muslim women at an Islamic rally in London. Muslim communities exist in most Western countries. Modern Christianity takes a tolerant stance and often actively seeks co-operation with religious minorities.

Below: Communion embrace at the Metropolitan Community Church of San Francisco which primarily serves gay and lesbian worshippers.

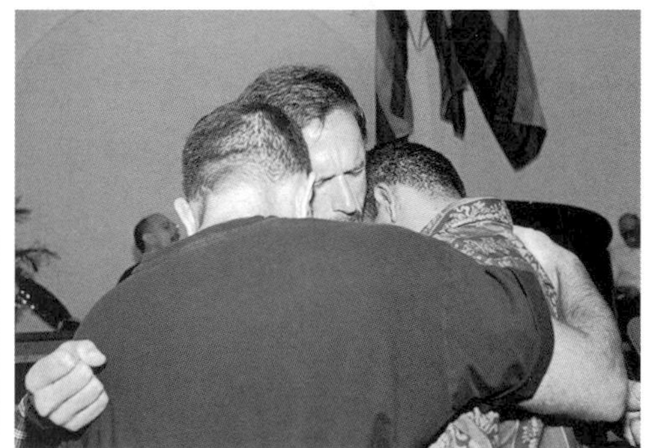

© Melanie Friend/Panos Pictures

© Panos Pictures

Left: In many Third World countries, such as Sierra Leone, shown here, multinational companies spend money advertising their products while the basic services, such as running water, are non-existent.

© Hulton Getty/London

the 'dependent' state of the Third World economies on those of the First World, which is held morally responsible for this state of affairs. It is notorious that increasing the levels of aid to Third World countries does not have the automatic effect of righting these wrongs.

The Ordination of Women

It is not absolutely clear whether the question of the application of the principle of women's rights in the Churches, for example, in the ordination of women to priestly orders, can be discussed in the same way for the Churches of the First and Third Worlds, not only because of the enormous social and customary differences, but also because of the vast differences in the way in which the question of individual rights is approached in the north and the south. It is true that many who campaign for the rights of women to assume positions in the ministry of the Church similar to those assumed by men, would assert that their claims stem also from Church tradition that has in the past given women functions such as prophets, leaders and teachers, long before some Reformation sects such as the Anabaptists accepted a female ministry. The demand for women priests is not a part of the argument about the so-called apostolate of the laity. It is in some respects a revival of older arguments about the status and importance of the priesthood, but it is also linked to totally modern arguments about feminism, without which the debate in its present form is politically inconceivable.

That said, it is clear from the historical record that the ordination of women to the priesthood greatly preceded the feminist arguments in their modern form. The ordination of women to the priesthood (as opposed to the office of deacon) began in some Protestant Churches quite early in the twentieth century. The practice accelerated after the Second World War. Danish Lutherans elected a

Below: Robert Runcie, former Archbishop of Canterbury, ordains the first woman priest in the Anglican Church.

© Panos Pictures

Right: A traditional religious parade in Catholic Mexico, dominated by men but dedicated to the Virgin. The dominance of female iconography in Catholicism is not translated into roles for real women in the Church.

woman priest in 1947. The US Methodists and Presbyterians ordained women on equal terms with men from 1956, Methodists in England from 1974 and Lutherans in the US from 1979. The ordination of women in the Church of Sweden in 1960 was influential on other Protestants, because of the continuity of Swedish Church orders. In Hong Kong, where an Anglican woman priest had been ordained as an emergency measure in the war, two women were ordained in 1971. US Episcopalian bishops who ordained women in 1974 found their action contested, but by 1976 this was no longer the case. A woman US Episcopalian bishop was elected in 1988. The Anglican General Synod authorized the ordination of women priests in 1994, and many such ordinations have followed.

The resistance of the Roman Catholic Church to the idea of the ordination of women to Church orders has been clear and consistent, as has been that of the Orthodox Church. After the Anglican action in 1994 Pope John Paul issued an Apostolic Letter confirming earlier rulings, and saying that the matter could not be treated as under discussion. Both Roman and Orthodox Churches maintain the tradition that reserves the main sacramental functions to male priests. It has to be remembered that 'tradition' in this context does not mean simply some sort of conservatism, but, in Catholic and Orthodox usage, the tradition that preserves Orthodox doctrine, and so the essential nature of the Church.

The question of women priests is sometimes blandly attributed to 'changing expectations about gender roles', a language that gives away a good deal about the application of social-science jargon to theology. It is not that, and the clearer-minded among feminist advocates would not say that it was. There were tendencies already apparent before the end of the Middle Ages, when late medieval Catholicism had allowed the rise of a new class of chantry priests, to introduce the principle of the labour market into the Church. At the end of a very long period of social evolution many Europeans and North Americans have come to consider the clergy as an employment that exists in order to supply a social demand: that female labour should be used is as natural as its use elsewhere. But most Protestant Churches would assert the idea of the ministry as a vocation to which men (or men and women) are called by God, and they would not allow the sacred realm to be appropriated to the needs of the individual and subjected to the laws of the market.

North and South

A century ago about half the world's Christians were located in Europe alone, without counting those of North America. The two thousand million Christians in the world today are very differently distributed. At the end of the twentieth century, the number of Christians of all denominations in Latin America, Africa and Asia is rather less than double the combined total of those in Europe and North America. Demographic change is likely to give Africa a steadily increasing importance in the pattern, although at the moment Latin America still predominates, and contains more than half the world's Roman Catholics. Nearly

Above: Wooden crucifix from Nigeria showing Christ with noticeably African features.

Left: An exorcism being performed in Legio Maria Church, Kenya.

Right: Italian Crucifix *(1955) by Sidney Nolan (1917–92), the Australian artist.*

© Panos Pictures

Left: Good Friday procession leaving from the church of Santa Domingo in Antigua, Guatemala.

Right: Archbishop Desmond Tutu, who worked tirelessly against the apartheid regime of South Africa.

Below: Father Dan Ohmann leading a prayer meeting at a Hutu refugee camp in Tanzania. The bitter fighting and genocide in Rwanda between Hutus and Tsutsis was a challenge to Christianity in Africa.

© Panos Pictures

© Panos Pictures

Crusade against the infidel upside-down in favour of the Marxists. However, the approach of Pope John Paul II to the problem was restrained, and in 1986 he said that some kind of liberation theology was 'not only timely but necessary'. The operation of this point of view on the ground in Latin America is likely to be through the 'Base Communities' , which are in effect parishes without parish priests. They can be viewed as a sort of compromise between the Catholic community and the trend towards evangelical Protestantism that has swept through Latin America – and also through the Hispano-American communities in the United States – since the 1970s.

In South Africa it could be argued that the Churches have come nearer, in the post-apartheid period, to claiming the social initiative and involving the whole society in a political process whose framework is overtly Christian, than any other Christian community in the present century. The Truth and Reconciliation Commission (1994–99) that has sought to reconcile South Africans of all political and religious persuasions, after the violence of the struggles of the final period of apartheid government and resistance to it, has had a very impressive degree of success. That this should have been so is due to the great qualities of understanding and leadership displayed by Archbishop Desmond Tutu of Cape Town. Political achievements of this sort are very hard to assess in the short term, and it is too early now to do more than to recognize the boldness and the great importance of the enterprise.

Africa has been in the past half-century the scene of major persecution of Christians. Uganda, especially in 1973, has seen huge persecutions, in which many priests and thousands of laymen and laywomen have died. In the past fifty years the experiences of both the African continent and Latin America have diverged so widely from the patterns expected of them in the colonial period, and their leadership has passed in such a great degree to indigenous clergies, that it has not been easy for congregations of European lay people to take these things in. It cannot be easy, even for a committed and well-informed minister, to convince a middle-class congregation in, say, Woking that it now belongs to something that can meaningfully be called 'a Church of the poor'. Yet this is an expression that has been used by many Christian leaders, including Pope John XXIII. As the demographic basis of Christianity, in a world increasingly affected by globalism, swings towards the extra-European world, the main Christian denominations are bound to reflect this in their organization and outlook.

In the north the big questions for Christians seem to relate to modernization, to oecumenism, and to pluralism: to ways in which life and doctrines are brought in some sense up to date, and to relations with members with other Christian persuasions and of other religions. But another question may lie behind these, whether the big future changes in Christianity are not more likely to come from the south than from the north. Whatever occurs, it remains true that what Christians have to offer the world is what they offered it in the beginning – hope. Was the hope justified, which the religion offered in the past to Christian societies? The question can be answered with an affirmative, as it can for some other religions, but not without remembering the long catalogue of error, failure and betrayal that accompanies the human condition. If we ask, did many individual men and women find their hopes in some way met by something that they experienced as a divine initiative, the Christian testimony is positive and overwhelming. But the injustices that the church was ready to tolerate in Christian society cannot be overlooked. We cannot forget the many millions, perhaps the historical majority of medieval Christian populations, who had little or no cause to thank Christian society for their lives, and who went to their deaths in silence.

1 Quoted in Klaus Scholder, *The Churches and the Third Reich* (tr. J. Bowden, London, SCM Press, 1987), which is fundamental for these events.

2 *The Christian Church in the Cold War* (Penguin, London, 1992).

3 Quoted by Ronald C. D. Jasper, George Bell: Bishop of Chichester (Oxford, 1967).

The great French historian, Jules Michelet (1788-1874), who saw the writing of history as a fight with death, pledged himself in The People to speak on behalf of the dead medieval generations of the poor, who 'like dumb creatures, suffered and perished in silence. Like the African who perishes of famine, they died without complaint. The European also toiled until his end was near, finished his life unknown to all...But these beings, who cannot make known to us their thoughts or their sufferings, can do so all the same by a sort of enchantment [of subsequent historical knowledge]. Learned men are needy for a drop of the sap that God poured into them [the medieval poor] brimful.'

Left: The hopeful face of Christianity in Guatemala.

© Roger Harris/Science Photo Library

Left: Computer-enhanced image of sunrise over the Earth as seen from space. The perspective of humanity's place on the planet has changed since Christianity began.

Reading List

The following books, as well as some of those mentioned in the notes, may be of interest to anyone wishing to pursue particular aspects of medieval or modern Christianity.

Chapters 1-3

J. Riley-Smith, *What Were the Crusades?* (Macmillan, 1992)

H. E. Mayer, *The Crusades* (2nd edn., OUP, 1988)

Peter Partner, *God of Battles: Holy Wars of Christianity and Islam* (HarperCollins, 1997)

R. Fletcher, *The Conversion of Europe: From Paganism to Christianity 371–1386 AD* (HarperCollins, 1997)

Colin Morris, *The Papal Monarchy: 1050–1250* (OUP, 1991)

Michael Robson, *St Francis of Assisi, the Legend and the Life* (G. Chapman, 1997)

R. Moore, *The Origins of European Dissent* (Penguin, 1977)

Norman Cohn, *The Pursuit of the Millennium: Revolutionary Millenarians and Mystical Anarchists of the Middle Ages* (Paladin, 1970)

Chapters 4-6

Euan Cameron, *The European Reformation* (OUP, 1991)

Eamon Duffy, *The Stripping of the Altars: traditional religion in England 1400-1580* (Yale University Press, 1992)

George Holmes, *The Florentine Enlightenment 1400–50* (Weidenfeld and Nicolson, 1969)

Roberto Ridolphi, *The Life of Girolamo Savonarola* (Routledge and Kegan Paul, 1959)

Peter Partner, *Renaissance Rome 1500–1559: A Portrait of a Society* (California University Press, 1976)

Nicolas Zernov, *Eastern Christendom: a Study of the Origins and Development of the Orthodox Church* (Weidenfeld and Nicolson, 1961)

A. Hastings (ed.), *A World History of Christianity* (Cassell, 1999)

A. Hastings, *The Church in Africa 1450–1950* (OUP, 1994)

Mark A. Knoll, *A History of Christianity in the United States and Canada* (SPCK, 1992)

Martin E. Marty, *Pilgrims in Their Own Land: 500 Years of Religion in America* (Little, Brown, 1984)

Chapters 7-9

Peter Gay, *The Enlightenment, vol. 1, The Rise of Modern Paganism* (W. W. Norton, 1995)

Peter Gay, *The Enlightenment, vol. 2, The Science of Freedom* (W. W. Norton, 1996)

Stanley Ayling, *John Wesley* (Collins, 1979)

Owen Chadwick, *A History of the Popes 1830–1914* (OUP, 1998)

Owen Chadwick, *The Victorian Church* (Black, 1966)

Elizabeth Isichei, *A History of Christianity in Africa from Antiquity to the Present* (SPCK, 1995)

Stefan Collini, *Public Moralists: Political Life and Intellectual Life in Britain, 1850–1930* (OUP, 1991)

A. Hastings (ed.), *The Second Vatican Council and its Influence across 25 Years* (SPCK, 1990)

Nicholas Lossky and others (ed.), *Dictionary of the Ecumenical Movement* (WCC Publications, Geneva, 1991)

INDEX

Page references in italic indicate illustrations.